ALL ABOUT
THE BEAT

ALL ABOUT THE BEAT

WHY HIP-HOP CAN'T SAVE BLACK AMERICA

JOHN MCWHORTER

GOTHAM BOOKS

GOTHAM BOOKS
Published by Penguin Group (USA) Inc.
375 Hudson Street, New York, New York 10014, U.S.A.
Penguin Group (Canada), 90 Eglinton Avenue East, Suite 700, Toronto, Ontario
M4P 2Y3, Canada (a division of Pearson Penguin Canada Inc.) • Penguin Books
Ltd, 80 Strand, London WC2R 0RL, England • Penguin Ireland, 25 St Stephen's
Green, Dublin 2, Ireland (a division of Penguin Books Ltd) • Penguin Group
(Australia), 250 Camberwell Road, Camberwell, Victoria 3124, Australia (a division
of Pearson Australia Group Pty Ltd) • Penguin Books India Pvt Ltd, 11 Community
Centre, Panchsheel Park, New Delhi—110 017, India • Penguin Group (NZ),
67 Apollo Drive, Rosedale, North Shore 0632, New Zealand (a division of Pearson
New Zealand Ltd) • Penguin Books (South Africa) (Pty) Ltd, 24 Sturdee Avenue,
Rosebank, Johannesburg 2196, South Africa

Penguin Books Ltd, Registered Offices: 80 Strand, London WC2R 0RL, England

Published by Gotham Books, a member of Penguin Group (USA) Inc.

First printing, June 2008
1   3   5   7   9   10   8   6   4   2

Gotham Books and the skyscraper logo are trademarks of Penguin Group (USA) Inc.

LIBRARY OF CONGRESS CATALOGING-IN-PUBLICATION DATA
McWhorter, John H.
All about the beat : why hip-hop can't save Black America / John McWhorter.
p.   cm.
Includes bibliographical references.
ISBN 978-1-592-40374-5 (hardcover) 1. African Americans—Social conditions—
1975–   2. African Americans—Politics and government.   3. Hip-hop—
Social aspects.   4. Hip-hop—Political aspects.   5. Rap (Music)—Social aspects—
United States   6. Rap (Music)—Political aspects—United States.   7. Social
change—United States.   8. United States—Race relations.   I. Title.
E185.615.M3538   2008
305.896'073—dc22   2008000816

Printed in the United States of America
Set in ITC Giovanni Book • Designed by Elke Sigal

While the author has made every effort to provide accurate telephone numbers and
Internet addresses at the time of publication, neither the publisher nor the author
assumes any responsibility for errors, or for changes that occur after publication.
Further, the publisher does not have any control over and does not assume any
responsibility for author or third-party Web sites or their content.

CONTENTS

INTRODUCTION

MOVE SOMETHING

This ain't the time or place for you to prove somethin'.
Cut the stargazin' yo, move somethin'!

Talib Kweli, "Move Somethin'," *Reflection Eternal*

The problem I want to address in this book reveals itself even in the words people choose on the fly. In Colorado Springs, there has lately been a spate of murders traced to fights beginning at hip-hop clubs and concerts. The local police have called attention to it, and a twenty-six-year-old interviewed on the topic said, "This city wants to shut down hip-hop. They don't want it to survive."

The word *survive* is key here. There is a certain drama in it. There is, we are to assume, something or someone working against hip-hop in some way that threatens that it will, someday soon, cease to exist. The idea is that hip-hop is not just music, but that it has some kind of larger potential. It is trying to go somewhere, *do* something—but is always just on the verge of disappearing.

Yet let's face it: The interviewee could not think hip-hop

in itself is in danger of eclipse; new recordings and mixtapes are released weekly and have been for decades. To him, there's something larger, more abstract, than hip-hop's mere existence: hip-hop must not just exist but *survive*, like some tropical flower or, more pointedly, a race of people.

You often hear people talking about the *survival* of hip-hop, and it is an established way of kicking off or titling an article on hip-hop. This interviewee has drunk in this pervasive sense in our culture, of hip-hop as more than club music and clothes, but as something that must *survive*. What does someone mean when he talks about hip-hop "surviving"?

Of course, white rockers are hardly unknown to espouse antiestablishment politics in their music. But no one is under the impression that their doing so is anything other than what it is. For a lot of folks out there, hip-hop is somehow different. Apparently there is something weightier, deeper—some kind of potential in hip-hop that the rest of us have missed.

Quite a few seem to think so. There are legions of people on fire with this idea: that the hip-hop they love has *significance*, beyond its volume and how much fun it is to dance to.

You hear this in the way people talk about hip-hop on talk shows, discussion panels, and in casual conversations. A lot of the titles of the books always coming out on hip-hop tell it all, for example.

S. Craig Watkins tells us that *Hip Hop Matters*. He is saluting Cornel West's book title *Race Matters*, with an implication that hip-hop is not just something to enjoy, but that it *means* something in a societal sense. Imani Perry's title is *Prophets of the Hood: Politics and Poetics in Hip Hop*: "prophets" who will, as prophets do, tell us something important. Something of even a religious weight, perhaps, as Alex Gee and John E. Teter imply with their title *Jesus and the Hip-Hop Prophets*, and Saideh Page-Browne does with the title *From Hiphop to Heaven*.

Hip-hop is not just music, but some kind of "force," apparently. Jeff Chang titled his signature history of the music *Can't Stop Won't Stop*. Catchy, but people are writing new chamber music all the time, and yet imagine a history of classical chamber music called *Can't Stop Won't Stop*. Chang taps into a sense that there is something dramatically notable about the fact that hip-hop doesn't stop. It *won't* stop—The Man wants it to but it *will not*, it *refuses* to. Presumably because it promises to do something that will make Establishment types very uncomfortable. Or: Chang's subtitle is "A History of the Hip-hop Generation." "Hip-hop Generation" carries an air of surging forward as well: a generation of people raised on hip-hop and as such, poised to do something based on that. There is, apparently, something *promising* about the generation raised on Tupac and Ludacris. Bakari Kitwana thinks so, too, with his *The Hip-Hop Generation*.

The idea is, more precisely, that hip-hop is going to be the spark for a second Civil Rights revolution. What Martin Luther King pulled off in the sixties wasn't enough. Jeffrey O. G. Ogbar announces the *Hip-Hop Revolution: The Culture and Politics of Rap.* So rap is not just music: it is, or has, or will create "politics." Patricia Hill Collins takes us *From Black Power to Hip Hop.* One may have thought that hip-hop was just music playing in clubs, but Collins's title ex-emplifies the idea that hip-hop is something more, analogous to "Black Power," a potential source of *political change.* Todd Boyd even gets explicit about this with his *The New H.N.I.C.: The Death of Civil Rights and the Reign of Hip Hop* (H.N.I.C. stands for "head niggas in charge"). To Boyd, the Civil Rights Movement was much less interest-ing, and had much less impact on America, than "the Reign of Hip Hop." To Boyd, hip-hop is a political phenomenon of equal weight to the accomplishments of the Southern Christian Leadership Conference. For these authors, if hip-hop continues to be just music, then a shoe hasn't dropped. To them, hip-hop is ever on the brink of going to some new level.

But it isn't, and this book is about showing why, as well as why that is not a message of despair. That is, we can indeed overcome. It won't be to a beat, and it won't be with our middle fingers stuck up. But it will be. Ladies and gentlemen, as I live and breathe, *it will be.*

However, there are a few things that this book will not "be." My experience commenting on hip-hop has taught me that more than a few people out there will have picked this book up with expectations that will go unfulfilled.

First, this is not a book about whether hip-hop is good or not. I am not interested in devoting a whole book to telling people that there is something "bad" about the music that they love, especially since I like a lot of it myself. Clearly, anyone claiming there is nothing good about hip-hop can and should be smacked down by someone referring to any number of fantastic hip-hop recordings that few people could get no pleasure from. For me, anything OutKast, the Stravinskies of rap, have done would be an example.

I do not out-and-out live to hip-hop the way many people do. But I like enough of it that I would consider my life poorer if it weren't around. Rap has been part of America for, basically, my whole life. I could not write this book about music I hated—or at least, I would not. Thus if you are waiting for me to rail against profanity, complain that rappers are untalented, or sound off about the vulgar imagery, you will be disappointed—whether you agree with those views or hotly reject them.

Second, this is not a book arguing that hip-hop causes violence or anything else associated with inner-city problems. My feeling on that question is that it does not. However, that's not what this book happens to be about. Those waiting for me to say that hip-hop "fosters a culture of violence" will feel let down.

Third, this is not a book written by someone who thinks all hip-hop is the kind 50 Cent comes up with. A lot of folks out there sit ever on the edge of their seats waiting to object that "it's not all like that," proud of their knowledge of the "digging-in-the-crates"/"conscious" hip-hop and ready to rattle off the names of some groups. Well, I, for one, know that it's not all "like that," as will be clear throughout the book. Waiting to pull out your Digable Planets or The Roots CDs as a response to what I want to get across in this book won't work. For example, De La Soul's *3 Feet High and Rising* is what I consider one of the gems of my music collection. I know quite well that there is plenty of conscious rap like it—because I have bought it and enjoyed it. Therefore, people expecting a book written by some poor fool who thinks all rap is Young Jeezy will be frustrated.

My argument in this book, then, is not just one more "hip-hop is bad" statement. It is a much more specific argument. My argument will be that there is nothing hip-hop music or hip-hop "culture" has to offer black America in terms of political activism.

By the way, I am talking about, very specifically, black uplift in the political sense: "revolution," as it were. Rappers certainly offer any number of observations that are "positive" enough, but unrelated to black America overcoming.

For example, who would think that anyone could come up with a rap about a man apologizing to his ex's mother that their relationship didn't work out, and much less that it would be a huge hit?! I am well aware of songs like OutKast's "Miss Jackson," and the fact that they depart from the drive-by/womanizing routines rap gets so much criticism for. But that song could depict people of any color anywhere: romantic relationships are hard on all human beings. "Miss Jackson" is seriously good pop music, but it's irrelevant to the specific issue of revolution for black people in the US of A.

So of course lots of rap has a positive message. You can't listen to more than about two hip-hop recordings and miss this. But my argument in this book is about one part of that positive message: the idea that rap has some kind of potential for fostering a revolution that will lift poor blacks out of ghettos and create a new day. Whether rap tells teens to use condoms or asks black men to be nicer to their ladies is a different topic altogether. More to the point, if those were the only things "conscious" rap addressed, no one would be musing about a hip-hop "revolution."

I'm interested in whether rap will, as it were, stop it from being like a jungle sometimes. Specifically, the jungle that we are taught that whites impose upon us. I am interested in how we are being taught to look at racism, oppression, the enemy we are taught to view as the obstacle to finally overcoming for real. I am interested in the *drama*— what makes people feel like the idea of a "hip-hop revolution" makes sense. To people thinking this way, what is foremost in their minds is not condoms, but white people, institutional racism, segregation, the "Power" Public Enemy taught us to fight. That's why people are so excited about hip-hop "revolutionizing." And therefore, that is what this book is about.

So I, too, have heard Tupac on the baby that Brenda's got. I, too, have heard Biggie eulogizing a murdered friend on

"Miss U." But my having done so still leaves me with something to say about whether any of this has anything significant to offer America as a political statement, as a *plan for action*. Brenda has a baby—and so, *what do we do to prevent more Brendas from having more?* Biggie missed his friend. So what do we do to make it so that fewer Biggies miss fewer friends? As opposed to just *feeling* for Biggie while savoring the groove?

If the message of this supposedly revolutionary music is just "Fuck!" the message is weak. *Fuck!* is tap water. I am concerned with what the "politics" of hip-hop has to tell us about where to go *after* we erupt with the idle, reactive eruption of *Fuck*.

And where does hip-hop tell us to go? Boiling down the "revolutionary" statements by rappers of all kinds and their band of chroniclers, one gleans a manifesto that goes roughly like this:

> The Civil Rights revolution only took us halfway. Some lucky ducks rose into the middle class, there are more blacks in the movies and on TV, and some blacks have risen high in the government—although they are merely apologists for AmeriKKKa. Still, vast numbers of black people remain poor and/or in jail, and the reason is that white people are holding them down. Racism remains black America's main problem, and the solution is for whites to finally come to a grand realization that there is still work for them to do. In the sixties the

white man only took one hand off our necks. The job of the informed black person is to rage against the machine, with the plan of forcing the white man to take that other hand off. Otherwise, we can expect little of black America except what it is.

That way of looking at black America's problems is considered as obvious by a great many people as the sky is blue. I, however, believe that it is mistaken, for reasons I will present. Hip-hop's politics are sincere, but its proponents are unaware that these politics are a dead end.

Yet my implication is not that the alternative is "Pull ourselves up by our own bootstraps." There is a third way. The manifesto would go something like this:

Black America's politics must be about helping people be their best within the American system as it always will be, divorced of romantic, unfeasible notions of some massive transformation of basic procedure along the lines of what happened in the sixties.

If that sounds strange or vaguely unexciting, this is only because a hangover from the victories of the sixties has conditioned so many of us to think that the only significant change is the kind that makes for good TV (and has a catchy beat). I, for one, am quite excited about the prospects of black America right now.

However, any sense of black politics implying that we

must seek some kind of dramatic rupture with current reality is a black politics that can go nowhere, misses opportunities to forge real change in the real world, and misses changes already going on. Hip-hop, with its volume, infectiousness, and the media-friendly array of celebrities it has created, is a primary conduit of this "revolutionary" brand of black politics, held up as enlightenment to a black America notoriously conflicted as to how to move ahead.

This is dangerous and retrograde. We are infected with an idea that snapping our necks to black men chanting cynical potshots about the Powers That Be in surly voices over a beat is a form of political engagement. We are taught that this is showing ourselves to have broad horizons.

On the contrary, this music has less to teach us than we are told. Hip-hop fans ridicule critics of the music as taking the violence and misogyny too seriously. "It's just music," they often say—but then at the same time, thrill to people talking about hip-hop as political and revolutionary. In fact, they too are taking hip-hop too seriously. Hip-hop presents nothing useful to forging political change in the real world. It's all about attitude and just that. It's just music. Good music, but just music.

The fashionable pretense otherwise discourages serious progressive thought of the kind that the old Civil Rights heroes who made our America possible would recognize. It clouds our eyes and ears with a dream vision of black America spitting verses so fierce and true that white America once again realizes that black people are America's biggest problem, gets down on its knees, begs forgiveness, sheds all vestiges of racist bias, and starts coughing up.

Folks, that's never going to happen again. That vision has no hope of coming true, and I will explain why. It's not only that there will be no hip-hop revolution. There will be no revolution at all. And yet there is no reason to see this as a message of hopelessness. Black America has all reason at this moment to be hopeful, and I will show why.

What we can be hopeful about is that change will happen. Not rupture, but change. Slow but sure. Faster than just fifteen years ago, even, but overall, slowly. Mesmerized by the idea that the only meaningful change in black America will be abrupt, dramatic, and will leave whitey with egg on his face—that is, "hip-hoperatic"—we miss signs of real change right under our noses, unable to see that anything is going on worth our support and participation.

We will not be satisfied just *proving* that we know life isn't fair. We will not rest until we are actually *moving* something.

CHAPTER ONE

WE KEEP SHOWIN' YOU: IS HIP-HOP REALLY ABOUT POLITICS?

We keep showin' you, and showin' you, and showin' you.
This is what it is!

KRS-One, "This Is What It Is," *Hip Hop Lives*

Well, okay. So what is it? When we really stop and take a look?

The party line is that hip-hop is telling it like it is, showing us where to go, hitting the sweet spot as it hasn't been hit since somewhere between Martin Luther King and Huey Newton. Ethnomusicologist Cheryl Keyes tells us that "rap music serves as a political forum," and that "artists utilize rap as a discursive tool through which to discuss social and political issues." Michael Eric Dyson, black Georgetown professor and today's most prominent academic supporter of hip-hop, writes that "when rappers argue over scarce resources for their poor brothers and sisters, and question why poor black folk don't share in the economic and social bounty of mainstream America, they are also behaving politically." Sports journalist Dave Zirin thinks hip-hop "has the capacity to threaten power like no other art form. When Kanye West said on national TV that George Bush doesn't care about black people, it created an unholy stir. If his stage mate at the time, the slack-jawed Mike Myers, or even another prominent African-American, like Denzel Washington, had said the same, the reception would have been profoundly different."

Keyes, Zirin, and Dyson see their statements as logic pure and simple. Yet I have a hard time seeing a clear relationship between the way they describe rap and the music one actually hears—"conscious" or not.

The question is not whether rappers mention famous figures and current events. The question is what the overall intent is. I think that the idea that hip-hop is devoted to political change is mistaken, even when "serious." Hip-hop is devoted to dissing authority for its own sake.

Why can't it be both, you might ask: why can't music that is all about attitude also be politically useful? The reason is that the game is at heart the attitude, making it too easy to miss what creates actual change. Activism and acting up are not the same thing.

ACTIVISM OR ATTITUDE?
THE ARTISTS

Hip Hop Lives
To show you what I mean, I will start with KRS-One and Marley Marl's latest album *Hip Hop Lives*. It's a good example of how "hip-hop politics" is not *constructive* politics, because the album is really all about the upturned middle finger for the sake of atmosphere.

As good music, there is so much to love about *Hip Hop Lives* that it's hard to know where to start. I like KRS's line about having been present at the birth of all of his children in "I Was There." On that cut, I like the way he delivers the refrain "Where were *you*?" with an intonation impossible to get down on paper but that articulately captures a tone of challenge; it's less a question than a jab. It's percussion. Verbal percussion is fun to listen to. "Musika" suggests a black-Latino alliance, and nicely rhymes *ghetto* not with standard Spanish *esto* ("this") but with the common colloquial pronunciation "eh'to." I like it when DJ Premier "walks in" and the rhythm track for "The Victory" is one of his typical spare, jazzy little grooves.

But if you listen to the album with your head rather than your heart, it's hard to see KRS-One as leading us anywhere useful.

KRS-One seems to think he has it all figured out: "We keep showin' you, and showin' you, and showin' you." But the politics are static.

"Employment is stallin' us," he tells us. The implication is that there aren't enough jobs for black people, or more specifically black people from the 'hood. That is, jobs need to be created for poor blacks.

However, at what point in black history has job creation actually borne any lasting fruit? Can anyone come up with two or three examples of where that was done and if it created major change in black communities? Not summer jobs for teenagers, although the record on that is hardly stellar either, but real jobs, for grown-ups, to work year-round?

Let's turn down *Hip Hop Lives* for a second. Down, down—hear those beats fading away. We'll turn it back up in a bit, but here is a time-out on employment, black people, and low education.

I know of three jobs-creation systems that are changing black communities. None of them are on KRS-One's mind.

JOBS CREATION PROGRAM ONE

In 1996, welfare was changed from an open-ended entitlement that basically paid women to have children, into a job training program with a five-year time limit. Since then, the welfare rolls have dropped by 60 percent, and single mothers have been getting jobs in numbers unknown since the seventies. Not as corporate executives, but they are working. The number of black children living in poverty took a sharp dip in 1996. The old chestnut that 41 percent of black children live in poverty is obsolete: the number today is 30 percent. Welfare reform was, in its way, a revolution for black people.

JOBS CREATION PROGRAM TWO

Around the country, organizations are giving urban black and brown people without college degrees aged eighteen to twenty-four the tools to find and keep steady work. For example, after five years of operation in 2005, 90 percent of the at-risk people who had gone through the program Year Up in Boston were still working. The program now has branches in Washington, D.C., Providence, and New York. America Works places former welfare recipients into jobs. Half of the clients have no high school diplomas; most score academically at an eighth-grade level. After placing clients in jobs for a training period, America Works remains their formal employer, helping the client acclimate to the work environment. Three years after placement, 88 percent of America Works clients are still off welfare. America Works has branches in Manhattan, Brooklyn, Queens, Albany, Baltimore, and Oakland. America Works was also, for the record, founded by white people.

JOBS CREATION PROGRAM THREE

The Bush administration (yes, them) has for years been channeling funds to churches under the Faith-Based and Community Initiatives program. One pilot program supervised by the Department of Labor called Ready4Work was successful at bringing ex-cons back into society and getting them jobs, with religious faith an integral part of keeping people on the straight path. Because of this success, a bill taking prisoner re-entry national is working its way through Congress, called the Second Chance Act. In cities, most returning prisoners are black men on their way back to the inner-city communities they came from.

To be interested in black unemployment is to attend to things such as the above.

And now, let's turn the volume back up on KRS-One: "Employment is stallin' us." This will not do. Is KRS-One aware that employment rates among poor black women are climbing? Is KRS-One interested in philanthropic, grassroots and government-funded organizations getting black men off the streets and into office jobs?

One might object that I am putting too much responsibility on what is, in the end, just one line in one rap on one album. But it is exactly this kind of line that has people thinking of hip-hop as politically significant, and it is misleading. When KRS-One raps "Employment is stallin' us," he plants a bug in rap fans' ears that black activism should be about decrying that there is no work available for poor black people—such that in the film *Dave Chappelle's Block Party*, a sweet young black girl, asked how she would change the country, says that she would have there be more jobs and gets applauded. But that is a mistatement of the problem.

Or how about a shout-out for the urban reverends counseling ex-cons? KRS-One thinks that the "church and synagogue are all deceivin' us." What he means is that we should be Muslims like him. But how "political" is it to turn blacks from the Christian church, one of its bedrocks of strength in the past and, to a large extent, now? As I write this, I am just back from a weekend in Atlanta attending services led by a cousin of mine who, with her husband, leads a born-again flock. Neither she nor her husband are after fame and fortune; they are not "deceivin' " anyone and are vigilant against those who might be. T. D. Jakes, superstar megachurch televangelist, is in his way one of the most powerful figures in black America today. His preaching and his message help turn a lot of people around. Why diss the church?

Screw authority as always—it sounds good to a beat. But this is not a recipe for political change, when church-based efforts are at the root of serious pro-black legislation.

There *is* work for poor black people. They are finding it, with the help of people who, as often as not, are not black. And meanwhile, jobs creation never works. America is a capitalist society. Jobs emerge where they are needed. In a capitalist society, those concerned with social uplift seek to connect the downtrodden with jobs that are available.

"That was real, right there" we get during a skit on *Hip Hop Lives* reminiscing about hip-hop's old days. But what on this CD shows any signs of creating a reality *now*? How to Stop the Violence? "A flower, a protest, a rally, a ban?/No, I got the baseball bat in my hand." A little self-contradictory, I'm afraid—or, if it's meant metaphorically, then what does it mean? Be mad? That alone accomplishes little.

Too often, if we take the step of actually trying to hear politics on this album, KRS-One seems to really be about putting his glorious self in our faces. Even in "I Was There," it's great that he presents himself as one of rap's griots, but why does he then become a bull in a china shop and knock writers who are trying to get the history of the music down on paper? "These objective rap historians trying to document hip-hop from outside, forget it." So Cheryl Keyes and Nelson George and the gang should just wrap it up because they weren't on the actual scene as often as he was?

I don't see KRS-One writing his own serious tome on hip-hop history, and if today's hip-hop historians folded up shop, then the scene would be set for people like KRS-

One to be ruing on talk shows thirty years from now, gray-haired and semi-relevant, about how nobody documented hip-hop's origins, just as today we puzzle over shards of hearsay in trying to figure out how ragtime and jazz started. Can only KRS be "All Skool," as he has it later on the album? The only reason to say these things is that the atmosphere of the music demands capping and dissing, not because it makes sense, or is even fair.

To KRS, his wisdom is so patently obvious that "Everything you doin' kid, we already did it / If rap was a toilet, I woulda already shit it." Funny line, but also demonstrating that the boasting is more important than the conscious message. "You know, we lead a movement," he says—that is, hip-hop is a movement, not just music—and "It's called 'I am hip-hop.' " And KRS's theme on the album is, indeed, that he himself embodies hip-hop on some level. It's all about him.

This is great theater. Theater is all about individuals preening onstage as self-appointed gods. But something this inwardly focused is not a "political forum," and certainly not a blueprint for a revolution.

"Brenda's Got a Baby"

Tupac Shakur's "Brenda's Got a Baby" is one of the songs most often cited as demonstrating what a genius he was, and, appropriately, in the artistic sense. This track refutes anyone who thinks rap is nothing but vulgar noise: this is, hands down, a poem, examining the psychology of a pregnant ghetto twelve-year-old with true sensitivity.

However, even this wonderful piece of work demonstrates why even rap like this is not as effective as "politics" as we are often told.

Specifically, it is a perfect example of how the "in your face" commitment of the hip-hop mentality distracts rappers from the real deal even when they are seeking enlightenment. Brenda's family are interested in her plight only to the extent that a new baby will mean a bigger welfare check. Tupac could see that this is extremely small of the family, but it is hard to imagine him rapping about how welfare policies used to disempower people by paying them to have kids while never requiring them to seek job training or work.

Despite having the same biological urges as people today, twelve-year-olds had babies much, much more rarely before the sixties. Brenda would likely not have had a baby in 1925, when even in poor black communities there were vastly fewer out-of-wedlock births, and even that number went down during the Depression. The reason was that there was no government program to support out-of-wedlock children.

I suspect, from what I have seen among countless blacks, including well-informed ones, that Tupac was not even aware that welfare had only been a program like this since the late sixties, aimed at poor blacks as a kind of riot insurance. Yes, welfare started in the thirties aimed at white widows. However, it was vastly transformed in the late sixties into what most of us remember from before 1996. That transformation in the sixties neither made headlines at the time nor made it into history books, much less black America's group sense of our past. Rather, it is likely that

Tupac thought that welfare had always offered payments for kids on an open-ended basis, and that the problem was just that there had always been some small-minded people like Brenda's mother.

Tupac would likely have laughed along with most blacks at the welfare office's posted slogan in Eddie Murphy's Claymation series *The PJs* about life in the projects: "Keeping You in the Projects Since 1965." But if he was aware of Bill Clinton's promise in 1992 to end "welfare as we know it," he likely thought of it as covertly racist—this was the standard position at the time among people of his leftist politics. Like so many, he likely had never considered the cognitive dissonance between laughing at that sign in *The PJs* and resisting welfare reform. Because—for him there was no dissonance at all. Rap is about dissing. You diss the "poverty pimps" at the welfare office who want to keep people on welfare in order to keep themselves employed ("Word!") and you diss white congressmen who want to time-limit welfare ("Word!"). That's hip-hop's "politics."

To Tupac, then, Brenda was, as a poor black girl, "invisible" to America, and otherwise just up against the seamier side of human nature in the family circle sense. That's the hip-hop way of looking at things: antiestablishment, angsty. But just as KRS-One today cannot see the death of welfare as we knew it as good news for the black employment situation, the hip-hop way of looking at things could not perceive, in 1991, what one of Brenda's main sociopolitical problems was: welfare as we knew it. In 1991, welfare as we knew it was every bit as important to the fate of Tupac's people as the police and how he got treated at stores now and then (as he chronicled in "I Don't Give a Fuck" on the same album *2Pacalypse Now*).

I'm well aware that welfare reform would not, let's face it, make much of a rap track. I am aware of one cut that makes a kind of stab at it, "She's Alive," on OutKast's smashing *Speakerboxxx/The Love Below*, actually weaving in interview clips with single mothers doing their best. But that one cut is just an exception, as are the handful of others in the whole body of hip-hop that one might smoke out. Overall, welfare reform is quite low on rappers' list of what is relevant to the black condition. It isn't spiky enough. It wouldn't make music that would sell. Fine. But that means that hip-hop politics, once again, misses the action.

Lost in the System

And while we're on the police, the relationship between them and young black men is an especially urgent issue in the black community. This one issue, in fact, grounds the whole conception of hip-hop as politics. Much of the reason hip-hop is now considered significant rather than infectious is that so many rappers have had so much to say about police brutality.

But the question is how useful is what they have said in terms of helping to change the situation? Hip-hop is supposedly going to lead to a revolution: things are going to be really different. Has hip-hop given any indication of this in terms of what it has to say about the cops?

Let's take Da Lench Mob's *Guerillas in tha Mist* as an example, although countless other recordings would serve equally well. The general message of *Guerillas in tha Mist* is that blacks need to, somehow, *fight* the police—or at least, get back at them with attitude. In "Lost in tha System," J-Dee is in court before the judge and "He added on another year 'cause I dissed him / Now here I go gettin' lost in the system." The diss in question was a suggestion that the judge suck upon his penis. This is typical of the attitude toward the police and the criminal justice system on a great many rap albums, including ones celebrated as among the best recordings of all time such as Ice Cube's *AmeriKKKa's Most Wanted.*

But if the idea is that hip-hop is "political" in the simple message that relations between police forces and young black men are often rough, then this is a highly static form of politics, especially if what we get over twenty-five years is endless variations on that same message. That there is felt to be a need to air this "political" message over so much time suggests that the problem is not an easy one to resolve—i.e., that simply complaining about it to a beat does not have a significant *effect*. It would seem that *effective* engagement with this issue would require more than mere complaint. Especially if we're talking about some kind of revolution.

Yet all we get year after year for two decades and a half from rappers is "the police hate us, so hate them back" while "hip-hop intellectuals" cheer from the sidelines that this is politics. Yet this is a "politics" that has nothing to do with *doing* something—or even suggesting what might be done. If this posturing is a "politics" black America should be proud of, then black America is accepting nothing as something: stasis as progress, gesture as action.

Out here in the real world, there are processes that have built constructive relationships between black men and the police. One is community policing, where officers spend much time on foot in the neighborhoods they are assigned to, developing relationships with residents and becoming part of the local fabric instead of being perceived as enemy invaders. One of most successful examples of this style of policing has been in Boston, starting in the 1990s: there is a reason high-profile accusations of inappropriate police profiling of black men never come from Boston these days. Another useful process is frequent sessions where police officers meet with members of the communities they patrol, in order to lessen the sense of the cops as an invading army.

Also, since there will always be some cops who are incompetent or rogues, and even good ones who make poor decisions in the frightening heat of the moment, it would seem that we would want black men to have as few encounters with the police as possible. This would mean a fierce commitment to, say, guiding young black men to available work, discouraging the misimpression that the best they will ever do is landscaping or fast food.

It'd be hard to say that hip-hop, in all of its "political" commitment, has a whole lot of interest in that. Hip-hop is about telling black men they can't get jobs, because hip-hop is, in its very essence, angry. That can't help us. Hip-hop is all about entertaining black men with the comic book fantasy that kicking back at the police is what needs to happen, when in the real world, there is not a single case where black men have gathered to do this and succeeded. Sure, the Panthers tried. That was forty years ago, and where are they now? Huey Newton is dead. Bobby Seale and David Hilliard are reflective oldsters. H. Rap Brown is behind bars for killing a black police officer.

And meanwhile, Bill Cosby put out a book last year with Dr. Alvin F. Poussaint, *Come On People*, that outlines just how black communities can help steer people away from the prison pipeline and into gainful employment even if they aren't interested in going to college. Cosby and Poussaint are conscious indeed, and not just in "making some good points," but in writing an entire book that is loving and conscious on every page. Yet more than a few people, appalled that Cosby is calling on black people to take responsibility over talking about racism, think of him as a sellout, out of touch. Why? Because he's not being antiauthoritarian. Not because he isn't trying to help black people, because he obviously is. Because he isn't sticking up his middle finger. Because he isn't hip-hop. That is, hip-hop *is* an upturned middle finger—which is different from really working on how to help people.

I know there is conscious rap that urges clean living, and we'll get to conscious rap in the next chapter, but the overall tendency is clear: using and even selling drugs is a huge part of the hip-hop soundscape. On *Guerillas in tha Mist*, Ice Cube's character in his guest shot "All on My Nutsac" is even a dealer. "All on My Nutsac" is, in itself, one of the best things on the album, a fun duet with J-Dee. But still, how constructive is a message like that? Is the revolution going to be that *all* young black men start selling drugs?

The simple reason that things like community policing and employment counseling don't make it into hip-hop is that they wouldn't be as much fun to rap about, or to listen to. That's because the sound and the attitude of hip-hop is all about noise—wonderful, raucous noise. Noise lends itself to rapping about the po-po, complete with gunshots laced into the track, the sound of prison doors clanking shut, sirens, the sound of a gun cocking, etc. Guns and clicks sound good set to rap music because the beats already sound kind of like guns, and gunshots are inherently dramatic. Think, say, of the tight and right "Careful" (the "click click" one) from the Wu-Tang Clan's *The W*.

But does anyone think that fighting the police, even on a "symbolic" level, is how to solve black people's problems with them? It's one thing to enjoy Tupac's cartoon idea of black men rising up against the police with their hands on their gats. But what about real life?

Isn't it, rather, that this metaphorical solution is only so attractive to hip-hop fans because the notion of fighting the police lends itself well to young men "spraying" lyrics in a confrontational tone over sharp, loud rhythmic patterns? Again and again, rappers calling themselves "serious" pull things that spell nothing useful for us here in the world outside of rap albums, but make perfect sense if we see the main goal as being confrontational and only that.

In his N.W.A. days, for example, Ice Cube thought of himself not as a gangsta rapper but as a "reality" rapper. Thus the reality in "Fuck tha Police" on *Straight Outta Compton*, where Ice Cube assails the police but admits gang membership. Did he want more young black men to join gangs? Of course not. He was just making a statement to the Powers That Be that because of injustice, we niggaz are going to rise.

But how are things going with the uprising in question? Four years after *Straight Outta Compton* was released, there was, in fact, a black uprising right in South Central L.A.—the riots after the acquittal of the officers who subdued Rodney King. It is now agreed by those of all persuasions that it led to no political change of any importance.

Rather, Ice Cube has since gone on to make movies, where he often presents a more plausibly constructive message, movies like the *Barbershop* series. In *Barbershop 2*, Cedric the Entertainer has had a set-to with a mouthy little girl, a niece Queen Latifah is raising. Cedric and Queen Latifah start going at each other in Fred Sanford–and–Aunt Esther style. They calm down, and Queen Latifah says she knows her niece is a handful but she's trying her best, and Cedric softens and gives the little girl one of the hamburgers he's barbecuing. I love that scene to pieces, as well as, for the record, the way *Beauty Shop*, effectively *Barbershop 3*, shows us a single mom who is supporting herself working at the shop, as all of the women there are.

Ice Cube got real. The albums were not real, and I'm sure he knew it. Not only did "Fuck tha Police" give us nothing to work with in the real world, but three tracks later, Easy-E really gave us a handful of dust in bragging about his sexual endowment at the end of "Parental Discretion Iz Advised." Then there was Ice Cube talking about driving with a 40-ounce freezing his balls.

All of this was entertaining. Entertaining in the jolly but idle Rabelaisian vein of that line "I can bust you out with my super sperm" in "Rapper's Delight." That was about as raunchy as anything you'd hear on the radio got in 1979, and I remember my cousins as well as the black kids at my school chanting the lyrics to the song in unison for fun, and everybody would just fall out on the "super sperm" line. Easy-E's comment was 1988's variation on the super sperm theme. But what espousing gang membership, saying you're hung, and talking about freezing your testicles have in common is antiauthoritarian sentiment, not anything "constructive"

And in general, "Cops hate us cops hate us cops hate us cops hate us cops hate us cops hate us cops hate us and we hate them" is pretty crude as political statements go. It has nothing to do with creating the dawning of a new day for black people. Yet this statement is probably the most prominent "political" one in rap music. It is too safe to say that it plays a larger role than anything else in keeping alive the idea of rap lyrics as black America's Declaration of Independence. Yet it leaves us nowhere.

A point I should make before we go on: there are some who will object that if I am trying to make a point about politics and rap, then I should address only the likes of either Public Enemy back in the day or Talib Kweli now, and leave out the more commercial acts in between like N.W.A. I reject that argument.

Rap's fans, including its academic ones, refer constantly to rappers in general when proposing that there is something political about the music. Writers like Nelson George, Tricia Rose, Michael Eric Dyson, William Van DeBurg, Imani Perry, Robin Kelley, Cheryl Keyes, Bakari Kitwana, and others do not primly restrict their arguments to the albums only the buffs and fanatics know. They, while well aware that some rappers like Lil Jon are largely irrelevant as "conscious" goes, are referring to hip-hop in general.

And this is because most of even the mainstream rappers have their "conscious" moments. These cuts are now even clichés, formulas, just like the ones about guns and bitches. A rapper who wants to be taken seriously is almost required to dip into the "conscious" well at least one or two times per album. The Wu-Tang Clan came up with cuts like "Can It All Be So Simple?" and "Tearz"; then there are always tracks like Das EFX's "Can't Have Nuttin'," Ludacris's "Hopeless," and Young Jeezy's "Dreamin'," or Ice Cube saluting Afrika Bambatta and Public Enemy at the end of *AmeriKKKa's Most Wanted.*

This means that this book is not flawed in addressing rappers like Jay-Z and The Game as well as Pete Rock and Mos Def. A book on whether hip-hop is useful politics that left out the rappers the world loves the most would make no sense, since they constantly toss their two cents in on what they think of as politics. Making sense about what rap means for black politics requires, then, bringing Jadakiss into the discussion as well as KRS-One. Upon which, I will.

"Why"

How about Jadakiss and his political moment on *Kiss of Death*? In "Why," Jadakiss presents a list of what we could call political grievances. In this one Jadakiss feels underinformed about the deaths of Tupac Shakur and Biggie Smalls, Kobe Bryant's rape trial, sentencing for cocaine possession, President Bush's responsibility for the destruction of the Twin Towers, the death of Aaliyah, the paucity of educational opportunities for prisoners, Arnold Schwarzenegger becoming the governor of California, crack taking over the streets, prisoners having to do 85 percent of their sentence time, Denzel Washington having to wait awhile before getting an Oscar, children dying because their mothers are at work and their fathers are in jail. "Why they gotta do me like that?" the hook goes.

The song got a lot of negative attention for the Bush line, but there is nothing to add to that controversy. The whole cut is more interesting than that one line. "This is some real shit," Jadakiss chuckles during a breather elsewhere on the album. That would certainly include this track, and the educational issue in prisons is indeed some "real shit." But overall, the theme here is that "they" (that is, white people, The Man, George Bush) are blocking black people's way at every turn. Black people are not responsible for themselves; it's always that menacing "they" who we really need to be talking about. The hook tells us that I tried to do it my way but "They sent me up the highway." That *they* again.

Now, however "real" that sounds, has this passive, athletically cynical way of looking at things helped anyone lately? In truth, the cynicism—the atmosphere, the posturing—is what Jadakiss is all about here. We know this because he soon drifts into wondering why he isn't as popular on the West Coast as on the East, and then before we know it he's bragging that new twenty-dollar bills have been printed because he has all of the old ones. This has nothing in common with questioning the appropriateness of sentencing guidelines. Rather, his delivery of the sentencing comments and the bragging about his money have something in common: in both cases cocky and confrontational. The guiding thread here is not political commitment, but a tone, a surface, an air: being in your face. Whether it has anything to do with black people moving forward or not. And usually, let's face it, not.

Yet Jadakiss's catchy rant is precisely what Michael Eric Dyson is referring to when he says, "when rappers argue over scarce resources for their poor brothers and sisters, and question why poor black folk don't share in the economic and social bounty of mainstream America, they are also behaving politically." And upon trying to identify descriptions like this with what these raps really consist of, I simply cannot agree.

"Why," in itself, is fun to listen to, and my reading of

Jadakiss is that the grab-bag nature of the questions, including ones about his own career, is deliberate, intended as playful. A spontaneous slice of the man's mind one day, unedited. All the shit that's on his mind, put out there. A good listen.

What worries me is that there are a lot of people being taught that there is something more than that to be made of cuts like "Why?" We will not overcome by sitting around asking "why" with attitude, with the implication that what we need is for The Man to change his ways. What, after all, since the early eighties when people first started looking at rap as a political manifesto, has the evidence been that this holds any promise?

It bears mentioning that the title of Jadakiss's latest mix tape is *Kiss My Ass*. Call Jadakiss "deep," but he gives the game away in that title, which is what rap is really about.

THE ISSUES

In terms of how rappers address social and political issues relevant to solving black America's biggest problems, we also see that attitude alone has pride of place over sincere interest in making a difference.

AIDS

The leading cause of death for black Americans aged twenty-five to forty-four is not gunfire but AIDS. Every year these days, two-thirds of new AIDS cases are black women. How does rap, so "political" and "revolutionary," approach this?

For every rap urging people to use condoms, such as "Skinz" on Pete Rock and C. L. Smooth's *Mecca and the Soul Brother*, there are two reminding us that AIDS was foisted upon blacks by whites to sterilize us. You hear this again and again in hip-hop: Kanye West pulls it in the "Heard 'Em Say" opener to his *Late Registration*, such a gorgeous piece of work, but tainted in his tossing this street-corner BS off as if it were simple fact.

Why? Because airing that paranoid us-against-them analysis makes for better hip-hop than the truth that serious scientists are devoting their careers to, which is that AIDS infected humans through a monkey bite. No one could even begin to make a case that the scientists working out the details on this are closet racists blowing a smoke screen.

Nor would anybody want to write a rap about people getting AIDS from a monkey bite. And that is because what is front and center in hip-hop's take on AIDS is belligerence, because it fits the hip-hop "feel." Belligerence is what makes the music good. But in this case, the belligerence is based on a dopey cartoon street myth, spread by books and pamphlets that sway readers under the impression that what is printed must be true, especially if it appeals to their gut instincts (one thinks of the anti-Western fundamentalist Muslims fond of conspiracy theories about the West who earnestly defend their claims by saying "It's on the Internet!"—or, in fact, Amiri Baraka saying the same thing in defending his claim that the attack on the Twin Towers was known in advance by Israelis). Again, the fist in the air has pride of place, because that, in itself, is the soul of the music.

Fine, but what about the black women living with nausea, diarrhea, and exhaustion from their sickness? Constructive politics: use condoms. Attitude: whites cooked up AIDS and spread it among black people while Church's Chicken was injecting a serum into their drumsticks to sterilize them. I'm sorry, but this is not politics for a people with any respect for themselves in a literate, post-Enlightenment society.

Drugs

In the same way, it's not uncommon to hear rap saying that you shouldn't smoke crack. But here we run up against what the hip-hop intellectuals artfully term the "schizophrenia" of the music, in that so much more of it celebrates selling drugs and using them. The N.W.A. routine of holding up "the chronic" as the champagne of the hood was an obvious example.

Now, it is true that rappers seem to hold off to an extent on outright cheering for the notion of shooting up. "The chronic," for example, is a joint laced with some coke, rather than a straight dose of crack (the term is also used for just a strong joint). Snoop Dogg's comic tableau on *Doggystyle* and elsewhere is about smoking reefer, not shooting up, and legions of rappers spit about the same. Rappers shy away from an outright call to become a crackhead.

However, they are less chary of rapping about keeping

people crackheads who are already there. Rappers often openly mention selling "weed" rather than harder stuff. However, when what is being sold is not explicitly mentioned, very often we are to understand that the rapper is participating in the good old-fashioned drug trade, all about a lot more than doobies. Young Jeezy's "snowman" icon, backed up by references to "snow" and the like in his work, is an example. Okay, Biggie implies that he was selling in order to get the money to be able to make his way into better activities. But what really comes through is the glamor of the selling, especially with him going so far as to give us a game plan in "Ten Crack Commandments," in case the rest of us might want to look into selling crack for some extra money.

Once more, rap is not about forging a revolution. It is about sticking out its tongue. And doing that is not how people have forged political change in the past, nor is there is any reason to suppose it will be how people will in the future.

The Ladies

Finally, we do have to touch on the grand old topic of rappers' attitudes toward women. It's hard to know where to start, and so much has been said and written about this that there's only so much I even need to write.

Maybe just a couple of insights from N.W.A. will suffice: "So what about the bitch who got shot? Fuck her. / You think I give a fuck about a bitch?" ("Straight Outta Compton"); "Slam her ass in a ditch!" ("A Bitch Iz a

Bitch"). Or how about a title like "Bitches Ain't Shit" (the final wisdom Dr. Dre left us on *The Chronic*). Tell me these albums are now old, and I say: Come on. We all know women were being dissed on rap albums that came out last week.

My intent here is not to jump into the long-standing debate over rap and sexism. The sole reason I bring this aspect of rap up *within this argument* is that whatever this misogyny is, it obviously has not a thing to do with helping black people. It is simply one more example of what I am arguing is at the core of hip-hop: irreverence.

Indeed, lots of rappers don't diss women. Some do so but only lightly: Kanye West's "Gold Digger" is one of the most amazing few minutes of music ever recorded, partly because West's lyric and delivery convey a certain amount of fellow-traveler affection for the woman in question. Ja Rule's "Never Thought" comes to mind as well, or there is The Game's "Wouldn't Get Far," which turns up the volume a little but is hardly vicious. And there are the duets when a rapper lets a woman give him his comeuppance: Ice Cube's "It's a Man's World," Biggie Smalls and Lil' Kim going at it in "Another."

But the general air of misogyny in hip-hop in general is plain. While it has nothing to do with progressive politics, it fits right in with, say, the "Doctor's Office" skit on *The Chronic* where Dr. Dre can't consult with a patient because "Open that door and you'll see his big dick fuckin' somebody." Hip-hop is attitude. Attitude is not always progressive, and here is a case where I cannot see that it is.

ACTIVISM OR ATTITUDE?

Because of what rap is really like, I see statements about rap's political potential as a kind of incantation. I think that to an extent, people claiming rap is "political" do so based on an ideal sense of what rap should or could be like, rather than the actual lyrics of rap as it is. It is also true that they are of a leftist political persuasion, of a sort that frames black America's problems differently than I do, as with the employment issue KRS-One flags.

However, in the end this means that I see the "politics" in hip-hop as, at best, a light dusting. I just think of things like Ja Rule on *R.U.L.E.* doing a "conscious" track with "Where I'm From," but then following it right off with pure gangsta stuff in "Bout My Business." This is "acting politically"? It's as if he only did "Where I'm From" as a justification for the main meal, the upturned middle finger. You can hear, on the long, tender farewell track of that album, that at heart Ja Rule is a sensitive, concerned person. But the medium he works in won't let him express that except in dribs and drabs.

We can do better than that kind of politics.

There is an old joke in which someone is looking within the light cast by a streetlight for a dollar bill they dropped. Someone asks why they are looking there when they dropped the dollar bill a block away, and they say "the light's better here."

The politics of hip-hop is exactly like this. Being oppositional feels good and makes for good rhymes spit over great beats. But meanwhile, black people's lives are improving in ways that have nothing do with sticking up their middle fingers. They are overcoming in the real America, the only America they will ever know. The hip-hop ethos, ever assailing the suits, cannot even see any of this, because it is all about that upturned middle finger.

The beat is better over here.

But what about the great things going on where there is no beat? Hip-hop, quite simply, doesn't care. Why would it? It's music.

Too often for it to be an accident, I have found that people making big claims about the potential for hip-hop to affect politics or create a revolution have mysteriously little interest in politics as traditionally understood, or political change as it actually happens, as opposed to via dramatic revolutionary uprisings.

Rehashing that too many black men are in prison, they know nothing about nationwide efforts to reintegrate ex-cons into society. Whipping up applause knocking Republicans, they couldn't cite a single bill making its way through Congress related to the black condition (and there are always some). They are not, really, political junkies at all. The politics that they intend when referring to its relationship to hip-hop is actually the personal kind: to them, politics is an attitude.

Attitude alone will do nothing for that ex-con. Efforts that help that ex-con are sustained in ongoing fashion quite separately from anything going on in the rap arena or stemming from it.

This means that if we are really interested in moving forward, then *in relation to that task*, hip-hop does not merit serious interest. Hip-hop is a style, in rhythm, dress code, carriage, and attitude. But there is style and there is substance. Hip-hop's *style*, however much it makes the neck snap, is ill-conceived to create *substance* for black people or anyone else.

CHAPTER TWO

THE WORDS I MANIFEST: IS CONSCIOUS RAP DIFFERENT?

And you will find that this perspective is best—check it out
These are the words that I manifest.

Gang Starr, "Manifest," *No More Mr. Nice Guy*

Some readers at this point may suppose that the last chapter missed the point of what the "hip-hop revolution" is supposed to be about. A typical take on rap is that whatever Paul Wall and Busta Rhymes are pulling, there is a whole body of "conscious" rap, also termed "underground," "alternative," "grass roots," or less formally "digging in the crates" rap, that steps away from the gunplay and misogyny and takes on serious issues. This, we might think, is what will spark a revolution.

I actually included some conscious rappers in the last chapter, on purpose. There are a lot of books out there and only so much time to get through them, and so many readers may only read that first chapter and figure they've pretty much gotten the point. So in that chapter I wanted to at least give some indication that my perspective on hip-hop applies to KRS-One just as it does to Young Jeezy.

However, some might imagine that my perspective would not apply to a wider range of conscious rappers. From the way these rappers are talked about and written about, you would think that hip-hop includes an array of gurus of penetrating sociopolitical insight, poised to guide us to the mountaintop at last if only more people would buy their albums. William Van Deburg has it that they are "organic intellectuals—gifted grassroots individuals" with "a profound, popularly accredited understanding of group history," "well attuned to the requisites of oppositional politics." Conscious rap, for Van Deburg, is "visionary," "frequently apocalyptic"—terms suggesting that the music points the way toward Big News a-coming. Apocalypse—i.e., revolution.

But when Van Deburg notes the "oppositional politics," he says it all. Oppositional is everything, with feasibility on the back burner. Conscious rappers commendably refrain from rapping about shooting people. However, it's still rap, and being confrontational is the foundational element in the music. Therefore, the politics of rap must be, as Van Deburg notes, oppositional.

Van Deburg is typical in assuming that this stance is the only one relevant in thinking about how black America can truly get out of the woods. But it's time for black America to think outside of that box, and not just in order to hatch up new ways of thinking about racism. There will always be some racism. No one disagrees with that. Our job is to figure out how we can excel despite racism: plenty of us have always done that, even starting in bad neighborhoods. Our job is to formulate and enact actual solutions to what ails us.

I do not hear this in conscious rap.

THE ROOTS ON UNEMPLOYMENT

Because The Roots have a particularly iconic status as conscious rappers, I'll start with them. It's not that I don't like what they do: for starters, they're from my hometown of Philadelphia—I get to hear things like hoagies and Mount Airy mentioned and street names I know from my childhood. And as far as I'm concerned, their lyrics are poetry, pure and simple—they barely even need the beats behind them. The Roots write dense straight-up poetry, such that it's no surprise that, as they say on *Things Fall Apart*, they have a big fan base among the coffeehouse set ("coffeehouse girls and white boys").

However, in terms of what kind of "politics" this poetry puts across, it seems to me that what it ultimately has to tell us is "Sheeee-it!!!!!!"—and that's not enough. I will make my case with two of the "fiercer" songs from their masterpiece of 2006, *Game Theory*.

"False Media" seems to be the one everybody finds especially significant. The message? "If I can't work to make it, I'll rob and take it." Because I am "a monster y'all done created." Now, there's no point in droning on that this "glorifies violence." What emcee Black Thought means, what you are meant to glean, is that society is so set against black men that poor ones can barely get jobs, and that it's therefore inevitable and justifiable that so many of them go "thug." But that's a questionable proposition. Why did so few black men go "thug" after Reconstruction, or during the Great Depression?

Nevertheless, Black Thought is tapping a widely held conviction about poor blacks and employment. Writers like Bakari Kitwana concur with insights like Black Thought's, such that Kitwana includes in his list of items on a hip-hop political agenda "the retention and creation of jobs for working-class Americans." Robin Kelley rhapsodizes over Ice Cube's "A Bird in the Hand" on *Death Certificate*, where a black man just out of high school keeps being turned down for service jobs, and as Kelley puts it, "It does not take much reflection for him to realize that the drug dealers are the only people in his neighborhood making decent money."

The problem is that the unemployment of poor black men does not correlate meaningfully with availability of jobs. A black man without a diploma who wants a job can get one. I state that not as a moral point, but as an empirical one. Here are some reasons why. The beat from "A Bird in the Hand" is now fading away . . . and now gone. Please consider the following:

An influential argument is that the relocation of low-skill factory jobs from city centers to suburbs or abroad created an unemployment crisis for black men. However, Indianapolis's black community saw the same rise in unemployment among black men despite the fact that factories there did not relocate in significant numbers. Meanwhile, New York saw just as many black men drift into chronic unemployment despite the fact that manufacturing jobs were never a major mainstay of black employment in New York. Two academic studies have shown that factory relocation was responsible for at most a third of the unemployment among poor black men.

Poor blacks themselves in surveys do not support the idea that jobs are unavailable to them. In 1987, only 13 percent of unemployed poor blacks surveyed said they were out of work because they couldn't find a job. In 1980, half of the unemployed black teens surveyed in Philadelphia, Chicago, and Boston said decently paying work was easy to find; 71 percent said minimum wage work was easy to find.

In the late 1980s, employment grew faster than the labor force. There were fewer factory jobs, but more nonunion ones. Immigrants arriving in this very era thrived driving cabs, cleaning offices, and doing kitchen work.

The Bureau of Labor Statistics projects that three-quarters of the new jobs over the next decade will very often not require a college degree and will pay good salaries. These jobs include machinists, sound technicians, electronics repairers, mechanics, building and transportation inspectors, plant operators, equipment installers and repairers, mail carriers and sorters, sailors, fishers, and others. In other words, the kinds of jobs we already see so many black people without college degrees in.

Black sociologist Alford Young, writing in full sympathy with the problems faced by uneducated black men, notes that an unfortunate contributor to the black unemployment problem lies in the behavior of many black men:

> They often say they will take whatever they can get, but a sentence or two later say that certain wages are wholly unacceptable. This seemingly contradictory talk is consistent with their statements about problems with certain past work experiences, such as the fast food industry, where some men eventually find jobs but abandon them (if not be dismissed) as soon as problems or tensions arise."

Other studies have reached similar conclusions, none written by conservatives.

And now we can turn the beat of "A Bird in the Hand" back up, because it actually could be a handy backdrop to a final point about black unemployment. A great deal of research has shown that one of the black community's problems is that too many young black men do not seek work that is available. Even in ordinary real-life experience, anyone familiar with inner city life among black youth knows that there is a tragic tendency to ridicule black teens who take jobs at fast-food restaurants, such that many who do make sure to do it on the sly.

Many think that it is understandable that black men

refuse low-level jobs. There is a sense that native-born Americans, especially black ones on the wrong side of history, should not have to settle for "chump change," even temporarily (one can become a manager at a fast-food restaurant). I disagree with that position but understand its appeal to many. However, it must also be considered in a historical perspective. Notice that almost no one was going around turning down "chump change" until the seventies. Think about how hard it is to imagine a black man in 1932, especially one with an eighth-grade education and no real prospects for anything but menial labor, insisting that he wouldn't work for "chump change"—much less being applauded by friends and the academy. If you are black, can you recall your grandparents ever mentioning this as a regular choice for black men when they were growing up?

What was different? Well, we wonder how the guy in 1932 thought he was going to feed himself if he turned down the "chump change." Today, of course, what the guy turning down wage work means is that he is going to sell drugs instead. That is a different problem than the one Ice Cube implies, of black men watching one door slam after another and finally taking drug selling as a frantic last resort. Rather, many men in this position could be legally employed, starting at the bottom and making their way from there. The drug trade provides a shortcut, and unsurprisingly more than a few take it.

Yes, most of them do not get rich working as low-level drones. In fact, they usually make less than minimum wage—i.e., less than "chump change"—as was recently observed in the bestseller *Freakonomics*. But they do this hoping for promotion later. Drug selling is a hierarchy. The white guy takes "chump change" as a low-level exec, hoping to become the boss living large. The low-level "thug" is not thinking that being one of the drones is the end-all be-all, but that maybe he will wind up on top. He thinks he might be like Al Pacino in *Scarface*—a movie people like him thrill to—rather than a workaday cable installer making a mere decent living.

Does Black Thought genuinely feel that poor black men are largely shut out of the employment market when he spends his life seeing, for example, black security guards, cable TV guys, and so on, none of whom talk as if they wangled their jobs against great odds? Often, when he is in the studio recording, the security guard downstairs is a black man without a college degree. There are plenty of jobs like this available. The problem is that so many young black men are unaware of the jobs' availability—or opt to take a chance on rising up in the drug sale hierarchy because that's what so many of their friends are doing.

And tell me that it is better for young black men to seek the off chance of becoming a drug kingpin—and likely go to jail for a long time because of it—rather than take legal employment and living a less dramatic but *real* life.

What this means is that decrying the economy for leaving out young black men without education is barking up the wrong tree. It isn't a position that can help black people. Robin Kelley thinks "Bird in the Hand" is really, really cool: here is "reality rapper" Ice Cube telling it like it is. But frankly, despite the passing pleasures of what Kelley terms the track's "thumpin' " bass line, the tale is *not* the way it was then, or the way it is now. No matter how much fun cuts like Da Lench Mob's "All on My Nutsac," in which the dealer overtly refuses to work at McDonald's, are, they are not depicting reality. These cuts would baffle black people in the old days, when, quite simply, a drug trade did not exist to tempt young black men away from coping with an unglamorous but workable legal employment world.

What we need to do is guide poor black people toward available work, and if necessary toward the training needed to do it. Remember—by available work, I don't mean mowing lawns or picking up trash, but respectable work like being a cable repairman. If you aren't into going to college, you can be a cable repairman. Nobody at the cable company is hoping that their applicants have gone and gotten B.A.s first. Rather, they assume that anyone applying for their jobs has not. Building inspectors are not assumed to have spent time in college learning about Shakespeare. If a sound technician spent four years living in a dorm, he's the odd man out. There are jobs for people without college.

The rapper, even a conscious one, is quite understandably inclined to shake his fist at the Powers That Be and assume that the economy is the problem. It may well be that you can't write much of a rap about training someone to fix heaters and air conditioners.

In which case, it may be that in thinking about how to get ahead, even the conscious kind of rap is something we might want to look beyond.

Of course, to analyze every political statement The Roots have ever made would require a whole book. However, the general pattern is that they trace black America's problems to a morally putrescent government, such that we need to think about a sharp rupture with the current modus operandi in our national fabric. I do not hear an orientation toward what could actually happen in the real world.

Take another cut, "Don't Feel Right." "The struggle ain't right up in your face, it's more subtle." I suppose. Black Thought gets more specific: "The system makin' its paper from the prison." So, The Roots are political because they cite the prison-industrial complex. Well—let's acknowledge that there are selfish, small-hearted people out there who are not exactly unhappy that the prisons are full, since they provide jobs and inflate the population count in their district. The issue here is what one chooses to focus on. Why not focus on the things that get black men pulled into the criminal justice system in the first place? Among people obsessed with the prison-industrial complex, there is a truly dismaying tacit assumption: that it is inevitable, and even acceptable, that black men will end up on the wrong side of the law. I gather that part of that assumption is based on the notion that poor black men can't get jobs, upon which see above. In any case, hating the prisons is easy. Thinking about what got the men into the prisons and how we could change that is harder. Guess which one ends up getting rapped about most charismatically, even by the conscious rappers?

The idea that we must accept that poor black men will drift the wrong way until society becomes perfect is, at the end of the day, passive. How valuable is it, to people who need help, to mothers who have lost sons getting shot in the head over nothing, to say, "This is how it's going to be because the playing field isn't completely level"? Is that really a game plan? Is that the kind of politics that would best serve black America? With complete admiration for The Roots' music as art, I cannot see that this message is more valuable simply because The Roots don't talk about killing people and don't say *bitch*. "I ain't seekin' responses," Black Thought says later. But I'm sorry: if this kind of rap is supposed to be political, then we are going to respond, despite the confrontational tone that the rap emcee, conscious or not, is virtually required to take. And in that vein, when Black Thought gets off that "If you ain't sayin' nothin' then you's a system's accomplice," then I can't help thinking: if all you have to say is "They're racist," then because this has changed nothing since the one time it did in the sixties, you, too, are just letting the system keep going.

However, I am fully aware that The Roots and the other conscious rappers are under the sincere impression that the Fight-the-Power, leftist perspective on what ails black America is the only one that could possibly be correct. I grew up with a very intense mother, and I remember one summer (probably 1978) when she required me to read an entire sociology textbook, so that I would understand that the conditions that black people lived in in North

Philadelphia were not "their fault." That summer I learned all about things like societal racism, factory relocation, and even the military-industrial complex. It all made sense to me. It seemed like an ingenious analysis of what on the surface looked quite different, and I immediately had a sense that it would be good if everybody in America had access to the truths I had learned. In the wake of the Rodney King riots, my first response in trying to understand what had happened was to read a special issue of *The Nation* on the event, and then I read my first book by William Julius Wilson. I do get where The Roots and everyone else are coming from.

My point is simply that from what I have learned since, that perspective today does not allow us to change the lives of the poor or anyone else, because the problems have changed since the old days, such as when that textbook my mother gave me was written (it was already not exactly a new book then, I recall). Because I cannot see how that perspective can help people, I question it—not because I have some problem with dreadlocks, anger, or Black English.

I must also stress: I am not saying The Roots don't do great work. I am, rather, offering a disagreement with their version of politics. *Game Theory*, if there's any justice, should go down as a classic album recital just like Stevie Wonder's *Innervisions*. I can feel that way without agreeing with everything on an album. The end of "Return to Innocence Lost" on *Things Fall Apart*, an aural vignette of black men's ugly experiences with the police, in fact recalls a similar vignette Wonder had in the middle of "Living for the City." And the duet with Erykah Badu, "You Got Me," almost makes me well up.

It's not that I don't like or approve of The Roots. It's that I don't think their philosophy is, in the true sense of the word, progressive. Their views do not move us forward. Apprised of what they tell us, we are not in a position to help people. We are simply informed that, well, "Sheeee-ittt!" The Roots are fine artists. But as to what kind of politics their art suggests, I'm afraid no poor black person would benefit from it.

PETE ROCK ON EDUCATION

"Anger in the Nation" by Pete Rock and C. L. Smooth on *Mecca and the Soul Brother* is a rich few minutes.

For one thing, it informs us that "*library* broken down is *lies buried*" and that television equals "tell-a-lie vision." Cynicism, as always, is the staff of life for rappers. And cynicism makes for good listening in an idle sense. It's "hot."

But in this case, the message is to be wary of books and television. There's a fine line between that and becoming the kind of black person who gets too much of his or her information from crackpot authors distributing their books on street corners and at book tables in the lobby at chitlin' circuit theater shows. For example, "*library* broken down is *lies buried*" is the kind of thing that ends up leaving black people falling for the idea that AIDS was created in a laboratory in the United States and foisted deliberately on blacks, or that the Greeks stole their intellectual heritage from "black" Egyptians.

And Pete Rock is hardly alone among rappers—*conscious* rappers—in taking this kind of stance about school being "white." Dead Prez in " 'They' Schools" on *Let's Get Free* say "All my high school teachers can suck my dick / Tellin' me white man lies, straight bullshit!" The idea seems to be that school is *antithetical to* a black revolution, in that the schools aren't teaching survival skills for ghetto folk. High school is, therefore, a mere "four-year sentence," and the track ends with a parting shot: "bee-yotch!!!" Now, remember, we can't just group this with the gangsta theatrics of Ludacris and that sort: Dead Prez are cherished as "underground." Their hearts are even in the right place sometimes: one of their recent albums, with Outlawz, was called *Can't Sell Dope Forever*. I agree! But I'm sorry— the last time I checked, having a decent fund of general knowledge was a big plus in forging sociopolitical change. What would a track like " 'They' Schools" have to tell lawyers for the NAACP who were central in the founding of modern civil rights law? One of them, Charles Houston, was known to counsel "Lose your temper, lose your case." Upon which we must note that hip-hop is all about losing your temper.

So when Ice Cube dismisses school as being about someone who "didn't give a fuck about me" in "The Product," some people celebrate it as higher awareness—but they shouldn't. *College Dropout? Late Registration?* I didn't think those Kanye titles were funny even though I loved the albums. *Graduation* was much better (at least, as a title).

I know there are some black people who consider grapevine theorizing, conspiracy theories, and unfocused cynicism a kind of higher awareness. I'm not one of them, nor are countless millions of blacks. This means that, at best, Pete Rock's position in this case is not progressive, revolutionary, or transformational in some pure sense that all would agree with. It is one man's opinion out of many— and not one likely to attract enough consensus to revolutionize much of anything. Lord forbid anyone tell my future children that they should read books with a sense of wariness and distance in case the book harbors some kind of coded anti-black message written by the white man.

And as for Pete Rock letting us know that "I'm aware of segregation," that's not as slam-dunk a point in the "political" sense as it sounds.

If white flight left a neighborhood all black, then treating the white flight as why the neighborhoods are so often hellholes is risky: Do we really want to say blacks need whites around to lead constructive lives? Did black men start leaving their children to be raised by their mothers alone because the Lutzkys no longer lived down the block? Are black boys shooting each other practically for sport because the Houlihans moved away?

And given Pete Rock's Muslim identification, surely he would celebrate the idea of black communities. Well, black communities are, by definition, segregated. So, okay, he's "aware of segregation." But I'd think in some ways he'd be for it.

When black politics are discussed, segregation also often refers to the idea that black students are segregated in poorly funded schools while white kids get great educations at schools awash in money out in the suburbs. If that's all one has heard, then understandably, one decries "segregation" and thinks of that act as constructive political engagement. However, there are things one may not have heard. Let's turn down "Anger in the Nation" . . . down, down . . . and out. Here are some very *real* things:

In New Jersey, since 1998 poor school districts in fact have been funded at the same rates as plush suburban ones and often at higher rates, with provisions for health care, after-school and summer programs, and technological upgrades—and not just in one city or county, but throughout the state.

Ten years later, only professional boosters are happy with the results. After decades of steeping in bureaucratic mire and poor superintendance by undertrained and underenthusiastic teachers and administrators, these schools could be made little better with money. In addition, the requirements ran up confusingly against those enforced by an earlier state takeover of the schools in three major cities, and then again in 2002 against those of No Child Left Behind. The schools have been wholly unable to match the standards enforced by NCLB, even though before 2002 it was considered a hopeful sign that reading and math scores were up somewhat for younger children (but not older ones).

In 1985 in Kansas City, 1.4 billion dollars were devoted to building twelve new schools in the urban area to replace the

shabby ones black students had had to put up with for decades. The new schools had planetariums, broadcast studios,
video editing labs, and Olympic-sized swimming pools, and
offered fencing lessons. Average classroom size was halved to
twenty-two to twenty-seven students per class. Per-pupil
spending was doubled.

It is known that education at early ages is key. In the elementary schools, each student had access to his or her own computer, and there were French and German language schools as
well. There were soon fifty-three counselors for elementary
school students where there had once been none.

The results? Dropout rates nearly doubled. The gap in achievement between black and white students stayed put. The
schools required security guards to combat theft and violence.
Meanwhile, white schools in the suburbs, operating with
much less money and no planetariums, performed much
better.

Say that the problem with Kansas City schools is still segregation and you are saying that black kids can't learn in one another's company *even in perfect schools.* Clearly, the problem
was with bad teachers, incompetent administrators, and children from homes unable to provide them with the resources
to perform well in school. How about rapping about that?

In Washington, D.C., spending per pupil is twice the national
average and school performance is among the worst in
America. In Cambridge, Massachusetts, per-pupil spending is

twice the state average, but performance is well below. In Sausalito, California, per-pupil spending is three times the state average, but the district ranks in the lowest quartile in the state in terms of performance.

Black Harvard economist Roland Fryer has shown in his work that the tendency for black students to be teased for "acting white" and to let their grades slip to fit in is common in integrated schools, but rare in all-black schools. Another study confirms the same.

There are fifty-seven KIPP (Knowledge Is Power Program) charter schools across the nation. Ninety percent of the KIPP schools' fourteen thousand students are black or Latino. Four in five are from low-income backgrounds. KIPP hires committed teachers and has a longer school day than ordinary schools. Discipline is expected and stressed. Eighty percent of the students who have come through KIPP schools have gone to college—from *segregated* schools.

And now back up on the thumping from "Anger in the Nation": "Some won't survive the next confrontation / and I'm aware of segregation!" Good for you, Pete Rock. But if it's as simple as that when people are black, there's something automatically wrong if no white people are around, then I'm worried about what kind of "consciousness" we're dealing with here.

Insisting that things are still so simple that black people need to get together and rise in fury against an evil oppressor makes for entertaining hip-hop. It sounds good uttered fiercely and set to a driving beat. But this way of parsing things does not correspond to what black America really needs today, as opposed to what it needed fifty years ago.

TIME OUT: POSITIVE VERSUS REVOLUTIONARY

As I have noted, my point of focus in this book is not just "positive messages." There are plenty in rap, and more than plenty in conscious rap. My interest is in the idea that rap is poised to create sociopolitical change, a revolution. In this, I see no significant difference between how likely conscious rap is to do this and how likely raunchier rap is.

We can use an act like Gang Starr as an example. They are well accepted as an "underground" act who more people ought to be listening to. After all, Guru comes up with raps like his musings about relationship troubles in "Lovesick" and "Ex Girl to Next Girl." This advice to be good to your lady is nice. But black people hear the same advice from roughly every other R&B song, about the power of love or how much Usher or somebody else adores his woman. The revolutionary idea proposes that hip-hop has something more to tell us. That's why it's supposed to be so important.

On that, I miss anything concretely useful in Gang Starr, such as in my favorite rap of theirs, "Manifest," from their first album. It's catchy as hell, with that angular little Thelonius Monky vamp underneath and Guru's poised, almost petulant delivery (which to my ear lowers the temperature on a lot of Gang Starr's tracks, but it works well for "Manifest").

"Manifest" has Guru presenting himself as the bearer

of a special message—all very "conscious rap." But what is its contribution to a revolution, something the "Hip-hop Generation" is supposed to get together and make happen? "I mani*fest*," Guru says, and one can barely help but feel "yeah!" But is that feeling we have at that point based on anything that said manifesting can do—for black people, or for anyone? The whole rap is basically a celebration not even of how insightful Guru is, but of how insightful he is *going* to be.

The track is really just bragging. Gangstas brag about shooting people. Guru, opting out of doing the thug variation on rapper, lets go of the gunplay—but he still, to be real, must brag, signify, cap—manifest. About himself, obsessively, like most rappers. It's good theater. But how seriously political, in the activist sense, is any music going to be that has to dwell in endless spitting about "me"? "Me" is one person. Politics is about a lot of people "me" doesn't even know.

Gang Starr had a rap "Tha Squeeze" on the *Training Day* soundtrack. A memorable line tells you to "Speed on before you get peed on." And on that, it is vastly unclear to me how "Speed on before you get peed on" lends black people a blueprint for where to go from here. Speed where? Given that the peeing in question is presumably a metaphor, who will be doing the peeing and in which circumstances?

What I hear in "Speed on before you get peed on" is the basic assumption that black people need to learn how to slip from the grasp of The Man. But what if black people really need help getting connected to available jobs? What if black students are failing even in well-funded schools, where the administrators and the teachers are mostly black themselves?

Rather, *speed* is a catchy word because it's about moving fast, and *peed* is cute when placed against *speed* because (1) it is vulgar and (2) it rhymes with *speed*. And let's not even get into how infectious all of this is against the narcotic beats provided by DJ Premier. Let's face it—*Mein Kampf* would sound good set over beats by DJ Premier. It could be recited in German over his beats and Americans who didn't even know German would find it somehow persuasive. Gang Starr's stuff *sounds* good. Those old school slices warm anyone's heart (or they should!).

But the fact remains: however good it sounds, "Speed on before you get peed on" is not a serious piece of political advice. It is just a sequence of words that sounds good, especially when seasoned with rhythm, just like "Life ain't nothin' but bitches and money," which I presume we all agree is not a political observation.

Thus yes, the conscious rappers have positive things to say. I manifest, however, that they do not offer much to say of a politically constructive nature.

PUBLIC ENEMY ON EVERYTHING

No, not them either.

A common take on hip-hop's history is that there was a Golden Age when Public Enemy was saying "some serious shit" and then the Tupac types came in pandering to the lowest common denominator, and it's never been the same since. According to this view, if gangsta hadn't come in, then hip-hop would have kept on telling precious truths and pointing us all the right way. A whole book has appeared making a similar point recently as I write, *When Rap Music Had a Conscience: The Artists, Organizations and Historic Events That Inspired and Influenced the "Golden Age" of Hip-Hop from 1987 to 1996*, by Tayannah Lee McQuillar and Brother J. Their position is widely held among rap fans.

Public Enemy's Chuck D these days has become one of the black community's wise men. I've met him a couple of times. He's nice and he has a lot to say. It's been a long time since the classic Reagan-Bush–era albums that Public Enemy made their mark with. But, that said, what kind of politics—remember, we mean politics that have a chance of bearing fruit and are designed to help people in the real world—was on view in a recording like *Fear of a Black Planet*? I don't question that the album was fun to listen to. But what political advice did it offer?

First, there was that revolutionary paradigm, such as in the proposition that black people can miscegenate whites out of existence by breeding with them, since any baby with black blood in it is considered black. Nice, I might add, to perpetuate that old slaveholder's policy, but never mind. The whole idea is based on the fundamental notion that something vast (and improbable) is supposed to happen. As is the name of the album, with its overtones of whites cowering at the prospect of blacks taking over. Good title in itself, but that *is* what it means—the cover photo, complete with military duds and shades, spoke for itself.

Or, American history has been largely four hundred years of "rednecks," and our job is to not be "careless" and maintain "awareness" (presumably of the kinds of things Public Enemy had to tell us) and "Fight the Power." But people running agencies reintegrating ex-cons into communities and trying to take it national aren't Fighting the Power—they're working with it, and whether or not America was or is full of redn cks, it's all we have until that revolution we hear so much out happens along.

And more: "This is a b thang and so you've *got* to understand!" But that's a me e that has worked less well by the year in America since ut 1979. Since *Fear of a Black Planet* was recorded, millions of new immigrants have come to America, meaning that the chances of black America alone ever getting the Fed's ear have become ever less. Yelling that it's a black thang got the white man jumping in the sixties and seventies. Less in the eighties, and now . . . there are other ways of helping black people. *Fear of a Black Planet* does not point us to them. There was no way it could: it was rap. Conscious, yes—but still, it was rap. Rap is about confrontation above all.

Fear of a Black Planet is just one album, but Public Enemy's other one most esteemed, *It Takes a Nation of Millions to Hold Us Back*, is more of the same. It's not that it isn't fun to listen to rap's Daffy Duck, Flava Flav, and I know Chuck D and Terminator X were sincere. Yet the whole album can be summed up by the kickoff to "Prophets of Rage": "I got a right to be hostile, man, my people been persecuted!" Look at that track title alone, with the hint of an uprising, as well as the title of the album.

It all really got laid out in "Party for Your Right to Fight": the FBI did in the Black Panthers, and it's time to bring their spirit back. The idea that in 1988 black men taking a page from Huey Newton and Bobby Seale and prowling around in sunglassses talking about guns would have done a thing for anybody (any more than it had twenty years before) made no sense except as something fun to set rap music to.

Say that all of this has to be taken "metaphorically"— with the almost cartoonish CD art for *Fear of a Black Planet* being a useful prop for such a point—and I say that the metaphor is, still, one of magnificent transformation, a whole new world, which we all know will never actually come to be. The metaphor itself is of no use to people concerned with making a difference in the real world. And say that the relationship between the albums's lyrics and reality is "complex," and I start to worry when activist politics gets too "complex." Let humanities academics sit in seminars musing about "interiority" and "signifiers"—while the rest of us lobby, say, for poor black kids to be taught to read with phonics-based materials that have been proven to work.

"Up with phonics" wouldn't make for much of a rap, because rap is inherently fierce, pulsing, edgy. But that doesn't mean that teaching its children to read is less important to black America than teaching its children to hate the police. It means that reading is less important than the police in *rap music*. I suggest that the real world is more important than the rap soundscape.

Public Enemy had positive messages, sure. They talked about black people helping one another out ("Can't Do Nuttin' for Ya Man," at the end of which there is that certain way of laughing that is deeply rooted in the black community but that had perhaps never been recorded so directly and lovingly as on this cut), and some views about the place of blacks in Hollywood ("Burn Hollywood Burn") that are outdated now but made a certain sense then. I don't know whether "Pollywanacraka" is supposed to mean that the *only* reason black people date white ones is that they look down on black people, or that there are *some* black people like that. Maybe it's a fine line—"complex" like the oft-discussed question as to what percentage of females the term *ho* is supposed to cover—but whatever. It's fun to listen to and at least distributes its sly contempt equally between the genders.

But there is little meaningful connection between the message on these albums and what it really means to save a community. Down with the volume on "Party for Your Right to Fight," and now here is an example of what does real work for real people:

Geoffrey Canada, community activist, founded the Harlem Children's Zone program covering a sixty-block area with a battery of uplift programs brought door to door. The mission is to provide poor children in the neighborhood with nurturing environments as early as possible.

The programs are tailored differently according to age. The Baby College teaches parents child care skills and is graded by the age of parents' children. The HCZ has placed supplementary teachers in seven Harlem schools to tutor students in reading and provide after-school activities. The Fifth Grade Institute gives support to kids just before the fragile phase of the "tween" years. Then, for older kids, the Employment and Technology Center offers computer classes and also connects young people to jobs.

TRUCE (The Renaissance University for Community Education) helps teenagers graduate from high school: in 2004, its students were accepted to colleges such as Harvard, Yale, Bowdoin, Vassar, and Penn State. Community Pride mentors Harlem residents in improving rented properties as well as buying their own. Meanwhile, the HCZ has opened its own charter school, and is planning a Practioner's Institute designed to disseminate the program's practices to other places.

Now, that is, if I may, some really "serious shit." And I'm not sure we even need to bring the volume back up on "Party for Your Right to Fight" with its Panther salute. The real world is too important.

I think I've made my point about conscious rap and real politics. To keep things moving along, I have not addressed Talib Kweli and Mos Def, but I am well aware of them and have listened to their albums, and I hear the same kinds of problems I have outlined for other conscious rappers in this chapter. Basically, their background assumption is that black America will only change via white America turning upside down again. This would include any idea that there will ever be an America with no racist biases whatsoever, given that there has never existed a single human society where such biases did not exist, and people throughout human history have made the best of themselves anyway, including millions of black Americans. Utopianism is not progressive, nor is unchanneled agitation.

A REVOLUTION FROM THE CRATES?

There is a logical snag in how we are taught that this hip-hop revolution will occur. Presumably, the rap that provides the spark for this revolution will be the conscious stuff. These rappers, I assume, are the "intellectuals" set to take us to a higher place, not 50 Cent and Lil Wayne.

Now: let's suppose that conscious rappers really were teaching us about the kinds of things that people can do to effect actual change. Let's imagine that there was a body of rap music that tapped directly into the frame of mind that creates something like a Harlem Children's Zone.

Even if there were, conscious rappers are a minority taste, something they regularly complain about. Blackalicious have their fans, but because they are puckishly wise rather than thuggish, they will never know the acclaim that Eminem does. To get anywhere near that kind of fame, any rapper knows that being "conscious" will only get you so far.

Listen to it from a rapper on the rise. Rich Boy has said, "A lot of the rappers ain't talking about nothing, so I was like, Wow, I could be one of the new rappers that talk about something real." But he couldn't see his way to taking that route too directly: "But I knew when I put out my first single, I had to put out something that would catch the generation's eye and that's what they like, riding on rims." Hence his breakout hit, the marvelous little "Throw Some D's." Marvelous as in a fine listen ("D's" are dollars, incidentally) in the charismatic sense. But suffice it to say that it is about the likes of "ho's" in the parking lot giving Rich Boy their numbers but whom he doesn't call, Rich Boy selling crack, Rich Boy with a gun, and, well, you get it.

But let's remember that the participants in this revolution are supposed to be the "Hip-Hop Generation." That's a problem, because the Hip-Hop Generation is more interested in Rich Boy than in The Roots. Cora Daniels neatly sums this up in her book *Ghetto Nation*:

> Those who truly live the music will tell you that, like jazz, digging-in-the-crates hip-hop is overflowing with thoughtful rhymes, political commentary, rebellious prose, and emotion. While I fully understand the differences between radio hip-hop and true hip-hop, it really doesn't matter. Most

folks will never hear the digging-in-the-crates hip-hop. That is because radio hip-hop is what sells and sells and sells. The reality is, it is the only hip-hop most of us know.

This means that people waiting for a Hip-Hop Revolution are supposing that the revolution *will be stimulated by the kind of rap that most fans don't listen to*. This makes no sense. If the idea is that we will somehow make the Hip-Hop Generation start paying as much attention to Poor Righteous Teachers and El-P as to Biggie and T.I., then the question is how?

One reason I ask that is that as far as I'm concerned, T.I.'s *King* is one of the best albums of any kind of music I have ever heard in my life. His attitude has nothing to do with what I personally am like, but the way he expresses what *he* is like just blows me away. There is a part of my brain occupied by Duke Ellington, Steely Dan, the Spinners, and T.I.

Now, if even starchy me, of whom it will be said that I don't know enough about hip-hop to be writing a book about it, can feel that way, imagine how deeply those folks out there in the Hip-Hop Generation must love T.I. and other decidedly nonconscious rappers?

I tend to buy music in big clumps at one time. For each type of music I like, about once a year I buy about a dozen CDs of that kind of music from over the past twelve months or so. I once did a hip-hop run at the Virgin on Times Square (sometimes I like to do it at the store rather than online, so things on the shelf I may not have been thinking about will come to my eye). I brought my big stack to the cashier, who was a black girl of about nineteen, very much of what I take it is supposed to be the "Hip-Hop Generation." She took a look through my stack as she ran the CDs over the bar-code sensor. She was a friendly sort, and told me, "Hm—you shoulda *been* had some of these!" She and a male cashier next to her evaluated each CD before putting it into the bag. I had a nice little mix going of conscious and "unconscious" rap in the stack, and the ones they got excited about and started singing the singles from were by Jadakiss, Ja Rule, and Ludacris.

That's the leading taste of the Hip-Hop Generation. And now, you were telling me about a second Civil Rights revolution based on hip-hop?

In that vein, a quick time-out. I make no claim to have listened to every hip-hop album ever recorded. No one has. To be sure, however, many, many people have heard way more hip-hop than I have. Many readers who have may know some "conscious" album with a track or two that addresses black politics in a truly informed and constructive way—that is, in the way that I have specified, about moving rather than proving.

However, I must state here that readers who use these albums to play a "gotcha" game with me will leave me unmoved. I am referring to hip-hop as it is processed by its entire body of listeners, the critical mass who would be a potential source for a political revolution. If some underground rapper someone enjoys along with a few thousand other people in chat groups is speaking up for grassroots organizations, or understands that waiting for a revolution is useless, then that's fine with me. But if that said rapper is an underground presence and is going to stay as such, said rapper is irrelevant to my argument.

Is there going to be a revolution? Well, if so, then surely that revolution will be driven by rappers heard and enjoyed by millions of listeners. As such, I address the conscious rappers who are most popular, even if on a secondary level. As to the truly underground, obscure acts known to only a select set, I presume that no one thinks a revolution will be forged on the basis of music almost nobody listens to.

LOTS OF PEOPLE WATCH THE NEWS

Is the idea that conscious rap will take us somewhere beyond just listening to music based on a sense that there is something really deep in black people being aware of current events?

I sense that rappers' fly-by mentions of public figures and things happening in the news is much of what has so many people thinking rap promises some kind of revolution.

Is it perhaps that some of these people are stereotyping ordinary black folk in exactly the way that they revile in others? These people are a little too impressed when someone with a ghetto inflection utters things like *Secretary of State, Zimbabwe,* or *economics,* or rhymes two or three words that end in *-ation* or *-etic.* Wait a minute, did he just . . . Let me rewind a bit here; okay—yes! Damn, man! *Talib Kweli watches CNN!!!!!!!!*

When did watching the news make someone a "prophet from the hood," as Imani Perry titles her book? A lot of us are up on current events, and it doesn't make us political activists, nor does it make whatever we have to say especially "prophetic." One is not a prophet to turn on a TV set and see that life makes some people better off from birth than others and then scribble down some clever rhymes affirming same. Real prophets go beyond just describing things. They suggest something larger, something more. They tell us where to go.

Yet people apparently see great drama in young black men of humble circumstances knowing something about current events. The quiet assumption is that for a white person, being an intellectual means making points with sustained argumentation, and possibly writing it down. But a black person is intellectual if he or she just says the names of W. E. B. DuBois and Malcolm X in a rap.

Indeed, it seems to me that a lot of folks out there are in what can only be described as a starry-eyed enrapturement at the sheer sight (or earful) of young black men from the streets making gestures of defiance at authority. I can't help thinking that for these people, whether the gestures change anything is less important than that the gesture was made at all.

Even rappers themselves often seem to see the attitude in itself as something very deep. Young Jeezy spends almost all of his 2006 album on the likes of "I keep it gangsta and dey love dat shit"—and then titles it *The Inspiration*, as if there is something inspiring in the classic gangsta routines he goes in for. That's just it: to him, subverting authority itself is somehow profound, especially when a black guy from the hood does it.

I can understand that someone who grew up in humble circumstances as Jeezy did might get a high from having a sense of control over his circumstances both as a successful rapper and as the character he acts out when he raps. But when it's professors, journalists, and activists who seem to be thinking the same way in the name of looking to hip-hop as a political tool, I worry that precious energy is being shunted in useless directions.

I'm not going to name names, but I did a radio show once with a rapper whose name one hears more and more lately. This guy's work has a dash of the kinds of things that make people think hip-hop has a potential to change things. Well, if this guy wants to be a prophet, I hope he'll brush up on his history: he sincerely thought that the heyday of Motown had been in the eighties.

He's a rapper. He writes confrontational music. Some of it confronts power, a ready thing to confront, with quick, tart potshots. There is long way from there to the hard work of changing how a nation is run.

My point about conscious rap, then, is that because like all rap it is based on a smackdown frame of mind, it is no more plausible as a vehicle of change than regular rap, because what black people need today is so much more than the smacking down of white people, institutional racism, The Man, or Jim Crow. Today, the smackdown frame of mind is not progressive anymore.

One more example, since I mentioned El-P: there is a spot on his "Dear Sirs" on the magnificently weird *I'll Sleep When You're Dead* that many, I sense, would see as progressive. In a hypothetical letter written to the Powers That Be, he wishes that "the coke and crack in the nation is collected in a top hat and force-fed to the children of every CIA agent." I love that top hat image—I take it that we are to think of plutocrats. But what this is reminding the listener of is the idea that the CIA hooked black neighborhoods on crack.

The truth is that some unfeeling CIA agents turned a blind eye to some crack going into some neighborhoods in one city at one time. Their interest was not in infecting black America as a whole with crack. Their interest was in what would provide funds for Central Americans fighting Marxism. So—they didn't have the fate of black people as the highest thing on their list. They weren't ideal in their sense of sociopolitical commitment. Big surprise. But it was just one city, during just a certain time, long ago now.

The idea that this seamy little episode turned black America as a whole upside down has been an idle distraction, narcotic indeed, for way too long now. Some CIA agents being insufficiently attendant to black people's concerns in one California town at one time eons ago is why black people were shooting up in Newark last week?

And it happened a long time ago. It can't be changed.

It's good that there's rap about real things (including by white rappers such as El-P). But sounding off about insignificant events of long ago is not what grassroots activism is about. Therefore, it's not what a revolution could be about.

In fact, why don't we take a look at what has happened when people from hip-hop have made some revolutionary stabs in the real world? It turns out that attitude does not translate as easily into activism as people expect.

CHAPTER THREE

MEET US UP ON CAPITOL HILL: COULD THERE ACTUALLY BE A HIP-HOP REVOLUTION?

Meet us up on Capitol Hill, and we can get up in some real shit.

Dead Prez, "Assassination," *Let's Get Free*

Check this out: in 2004, P. Diddy spearheaded a voter registration campaign and called it "Vote or Die." Never mind how little came of it. As far as Nas was concerned, it was a sellout operation. Here was Nas's considered opinion:

> Hip-Hop is not "Vote or Die." That's not Hip-Hop. No disrespect to Diddy and Russell and them—those are my heroes—but Hip-Hop is not "Vote or Die" . . . Hip-Hop is anti-establishment. Ice Cube and them were always that way. In order for Hip-Hop to change our point of view, it means for us to have a candidate that understands Hip-Hop. If you say "Vote or Die" then you are saying it's all good that Anheuser-Busch supports "Vote or Die."

So, hip-hop politics denies the legitimacy of the way America operates and always will—i.e., real politics. Hip-hop stands outside of the political establishment, seeking a brand-new day.

Nas has no reason to think that politics of that brand has the slightest chance of helping the black people he raps about. The only way a recreationally radical stance such as his makes any kind of sense is that hip-hop is not about politics at all—it is about being oppositional regardless of the outcome.

This is why the Hip-Hop Revolution never seems to actually happen, and never could.

One response to the previous chapters could be that whatever disjunctions there happen to be between what rappers say and what a constructive politics would be, there remains a certain precious energy in hip-hop, worth trying to channel somehow. The idea would be that hip-hop is valuable in teaching people to question, to think more broadly than their own lives.

Thus Michael Eric Dyson hopes that hip-hop can "play a vital role in inspiring young folk to become politically astute human beings and citizens" and notes that "it can help alter the mind-set of the masses; it can help create awareness of the need for social change; it can help dramatize injustice; and it can help articulate the disenchantment of significant segments of the citizenry."

But what Dyson here means by "politically astute" is, I take from the imperatives in his work overall, indignantly leftist. America is a profoundly racist society in which black people's concerns are "unheard," and what needs to happen is white people "finally listening" and effecting vast transformations in the American social structure.

Dyson, in this assumption, is among legions. The idea among these legions is that we will be home only when the Establishment will at last just *listen* and *realize* and *admit*— and then overhaul. I suspect this idea of black people as "unheard" is part of what makes people who think this way entertain the notion that hip-hop can be politically transformative. The music is loud. It's hard not to hear it. Hence the resonance of the title of Tricia Rose's now classic book on hip-hop *Black Noise*.

People like Dyson, Rose, and so many others sincerely believe that this brand of politics is the only informed or compassionate one. However, my take on the situation does not support this view. It would seem to me that the issue is this one, and only this one: what kind politics have helped people?

And in that light I cannot see how the us-against-them model of politics has done much for black people since the sixties. If the politics that helped people in 2008 happened to be the politics chanted in music that feels good to move to and is rapped by guys who sound like your cousin Darnell, it would be a happy accident—and I would be right behind it. But that accident has not occurred. The politics that helps people today, as opposed to in the sixties, is quite different from anything much that phat beats and "attitude" have to tell us.

One way we know this is, in fact, recent history. For something that's supposed to be a movement, it's hard to see much actual movement in hip-hop's ever imminent promise of becoming a political force. Let's look at what has happened so far when people have actually tried to create a "hip-hop politics."

THE HIP-HOP REVOLUTION: HOW'S THAT BEEN GOING?

School Funding

As I noted in the previous chapter, there is a great deal of evidence that funding is not an important reason why schools fail to teach black kids (remember Kansas City?). There is, rather, a great deal of evidence that the problem is with underqualified teachers whom it is very difficult to fire, apathetic principals, and inadequate procedures for dealing with disruptive or violent students.

Notice that none of those last three things is easily traceable to white people not liking black people, even "systemically" or "institutionally." However, the idea that schools would improve if only granted funds fits well into the hip-hop ethos: indignation, disenchantment, playing the underdog.

Thus the signature achievement of the Hip-Hop Summit Action Network (HSAN), founded by Russell Simmons, was that in 2005, they sponsored a rally in conjunction with some other organizations protesting New York mayor Michael Bloomberg's intention to cut 300 million dollars from the New York City school budget.

Bloomberg backtracked, and this seems to have given a lot of people an idea that hip-hop really is about to become "a political tool."

However, the evidence that funding itself is not the issue is so very strong that, in combination with the history of the New York City public school system over the past forty years, I feel confident in saying that this money, mostly going into teachers' salaries, is not going to make a significant difference in how well children are educated. Money will not change the bad habits and the indifference that are the actual problems. Visiting a bad city school and then visiting a successful charter school educating the same kinds of kids, no human being could retain the idea that the problem at the bad school was cash.

Recently I met with the chancellor of the New York City school system, Joel Klein. He is deeply concerned with the state of the schools in the city and has spent several years working hard to make them better. The HSAN episode, in terms of the impact that little 300 million had upon the problems in New York City schools, was something he did not even recall. He was busy doing real work.

Or, here are some other observations:

One of the best public schools in the nation is the Frederick Douglass Academy in Harlem: 95 percent of its students go to college, and almost all of them are from gritty neighborhoods. Yet it gets much less money than lower-performing schools nearby.

The per-pupil spending rate in New York State is higher than anywhere else in the nation except Washington, D.C.

From 1997 to 2002, funding for the New York State school system went from 8.8 billion dollars to 12.5 billion. The only thing that happened was a tiny tick upward in fourth-graders' reading (but not math) scores. Overall, the situation remained lousy. That was a 3.7-billion-dollar increase. The HSAN rally was sparked by a court case proposing a 5.6-billion-dollar increase, a figure that was created randomly. No one arguing for this increase could have explained why 5.6 billion was going to have more of an effect than 3.7 had (not).

The issue in schools is not money, but how it is spent. Teachers themselves, even in lousy schools, will often readily acknowledge this.

But HSAN did not—*could* not—acknowledge that, since hip-hop is by definition about protest. HSAN can't agitate for New York State to allow more charter schools, because even though this would be a pro-black policy, it lacks the drama of agitating for mo' money for the old schools. Hip-hop is, by definition, dramatic. Getting black kids better educated will not be.

Poor students learn to read best with programs teaching them how to sound out words (phonics-based), rather than ones nudging them into recognizing whole words as chunks. Yet many New York schools have resisted phonics in favor of assorted touchy-feely approaches that have never proven their mettle. But HSAN can't go to the streets about that, because it would mean battling teachers, many of whom are black, and again, no drama.

Truth to tell, one sensed little indication among people who cheered HSAN on in 2005 that they happened to follow education policy very closely, and certainly not that they were interested enough in the subject to come upon facts speaking against their sense that funding is the main issue, or even an issue at all. We all have different interests. But this means that the Hip-Hop Revolution's platform on education would miss what the real problems are.

Bakari Kitwana in his *The Hip Hop Generation* presents just such a platform, and his issue is, predictably, funding disparities. That issue fits nicely the spirit of spiky in-your-face rap. But that spirit, in this case, does not help black kids learn.

The Rockefeller Laws

The Rockefeller Laws in New York State make the penalty for selling two ounces or more of hard drugs, and possessing four ounces or more, equivalent to the one for second-degree murder. In 2003, Russell Simmons joined high-level negotiations over shortening the sentences the Rockefeller Laws require. "Meet us up on Capitol Hill, and we can get up in some real shit," Dead Prez rapped in 2000. Dead Prez are conscious rappers, sounding off memorably in the film *Dave Chappelle's Block Party*, which chronicled a conscious rap street concert.

Well, three years later, Mr. Simmons Goes to Albany.

I, for one, salute the intent. I think the Rockefeller Laws, and the later ones penalizing selling crack more heavily than selling powdered cocaine, plus the entire War on Drugs, should all be repealed with all deliberate speed. (How's that from me, the right wing's darling black "conservative"?) All of this has destroyed black communities. By creating a vast markup on hard drugs' cost, these policies have created a standing temptation for blacks to step outside of legal employment, leading to generations of inner city blacks who see selling drugs as ordinary. The vast disproportion of black prisoners these policies have created undergirds a sense throughout the black community of the police as an enemy, and also preserves a sense that racism remains black America's main problem. Point to Condoleezza Rice and Oprah, and countless smart people will object that half the men in prison are black. In fact, if there had never been the Rockefeller Laws, gangsta rap might never have come to exist, and one wonders what a great many of today's rappers would "spit" about.

The question in summer 2003, however, was whether hip-hop could have anything significant to do with the gradual and intricate legal and political negotiations involved in repealing or tempering a long established set of policies with a fiercely vocal constituency behind them. Just a visual image leads to that question. There in Governor Pataki's office were Pataki, Senate majority leader Joseph Bruno, Assembly speaker Sheldon Silver—and Russell Simmons? What, exactly, was he supposed to be accomplishing?

His presence made sense to Hip-Hop Revolution fans. S. Craig Watkins notes that the idea was that Simmons was an "urban market guru, someone who understood the tastes, tempo, and temperament of urban life and, especially, its most dominant force, hip hop." All of that was certainly true about Simmons. But was any of it really meaningful in terms of getting things done in a capitol building? Those who thought it was were espousing that idea we have seen in this book, that there is something about hip-hop beyond music, attitude, and style—that it has some kind of transformational power, that there was some "message" Simmons could give these leaders. I take it that the message would be about how hard ghetto people have it, how hard it is on kids not to grow up with fathers—that would melt the hearts of hundreds of legislators and create change.

It didn't work.

They made nice with Simmons and left him thinking something important had happened, but the second his back was turned they let everything fall apart. Street cred did not translate into legislative influence.

And was that really a surprise? Simmons tried his best. But there are some sociopolitical situations that only change gradually, as the result of shifts in the public consciousness, chance events nudging the shifts along, and multiple organizations sitting ever at the ready to do nudging of their own.

Imagine, for instance, if Salt-N-Pepa were together today and decided to start meeting with legislators to work against the possible repeal of *Roe v. Wade*. Sentiments run a mile high on abortion, and there are countless organizations and constituencies for and against it working like gangbusters 24/7. We assume that a rapper or two showing up and having some conversations with legislators could only be a drop in the bucket. What new or especially influential opinions could a rapper have to contribute? Nobody would think of Salt-N-Pepa as a secret weapon, worthy of close observation because they had "street cred." Because they would be rappers, and rap is just music.

The fact that rappers actually rap about people affected by the Rockefeller Laws does not make Simmons's stab at activism different. In the end, laws, to whomever they apply, are made and unmade by politicians in suits and ties, answerable to local constituencies. Many of these politicians are trained in the law; they have known one another forever, and all of them are deeply steeped in arcane governmental customs. Then someone untrained in the law, whom none of them has ever met, walks in with—*Whoa!!!!*—street cred.

Only in a movie would this lead to anything important. Perhaps with Jamie Foxx playing a rapper, who once did the "gangsta" thing but, getting a little older, starts to get a sense of responsibility and manages to convince New York State to repeal the Rockefeller Laws while simultaneously romancing Faune Chambers. He takes a clueless white assemblyman (Steve Carell) on a tour of the ghetto, where they meet a mom played by Jenifer Lewis, standing tall but heartbroken by her son's being up the river for fifteen years, the son done by Larenz Tate. When the law's repeal is announced, the gallery in the statehouse erupts in a big "Hooray!" There is a quick shot of Bernie Mac, playing Foxx's promoter, giving a high five to Paul Giamatti, Steve Carell's aide who saw the light when Bernie Mac took him to a hip-hop club and got him laid with a bartendress played by Rihanna. Then the camera pans upward and the music on the soundtrack surges. One last scene wrapping some things up between Foxx and Chambers, and then the ending credits roll over a rap written for the film by Nas, its chorus sung by Chrisette Michele.

And now back to real life. Is hip-hop really ready for the long, slow, undramatic work that changing laws requires in real life? Or is hip-hop—quick, fast, and dramatic to its core—just music?

Rallies and Voter Registration

The main presence of HSAN since its founding has been in the form of rallies, where rappers perform and attendees are registered to vote. The official version is that all or at least most of the people registered then go out and vote. However, the evidence so far is that these rallies are not having a significant effect on how many people in the "Hip-Hop Generation" vote. To put it another way, as I write, there has been no election in which there was a new bloc of votes traceable to hip-hop rallies. Yes, over 51 percent of people eighteen to twenty-nine voted in 2004 compared to the 42 percent who had four years before. But then, overall voter turnout was up that year, clearly because of the uniquely contentious issues surrounding the war in Iraq and the Bush administration. A big uptick in the youth vote *alone* would make sense as possibly due to HSAN—but we haven't seen it.

Getting out the vote is not just a matter of getting someone who came to see Kanye and Jay-Z to sign his or her name and address on a piece of paper. Getting out the vote requires local organizations settling into communities and holding subsequent events up to and *on* the day of the vote. Remember the folks getting out the vote for Al Gore in 2000 practically dragging people out of their houses to cast a vote?

That's how much it takes, dragging people out of their houses. It always has: ethnic white political machines were doing this way back in the 1800s. Most human beings are not political and never have been, and don't see how their pulling the lever could possibly affect anything. If you are on fire with a cause, you have to *work* to make people even *fake* being political for a brief spell. You have to *bring out the vote*. HSAN, so far, has not gotten to that. Contrary to what many romantically expect, the charisma of rappers' performances does not translate into actually *bringing out the vote*. That is: getting out the vote is not that easy. It takes the same grinding, undramatic work that it has always taken.

Rosa Clemente, New York activist, in a nasty tone that I do not see the necessity of, sharply challenged Simmons's quest to be the leader of hip-hop. Simmons has sincerely tried to do good. However, she did get in an important question: "How many fund-raisers have you held for the numerous grassroots organizations?" The reason it does not occur to Simmons to even familiarize himself with who is actually doing what in the real world is his basic idea, shared by so many people excited about hip-hop being a "movement," that political change in black America is going to be about celebrities, phat beats, big news, drama. Simmons is one of the world's best impresarios. Unsurprisingly, he thinks of black America's future in the terms of a show. But shows, so far, don't seem to hold out much promise of doing any real good for us.

S. Craig Watkins gets down the issue here in noting that "A hip-hop political agenda that *matters* needs to be more strategically focused and requires people willing to do the messy work that emphasizes substantive change over publicity-seeking media events." Watkins, while no polemicist, is honest enough to clearly note that "as noble as their intentions may be, Simmons and Chavis Muhummad [HSAN's CEO and president] represent a brand of politics that, ultimately, is of little use to hip hop."

I would add, "of little use to black America," which is also Watkins's implication elsewhere in his text. I also suggest that if the genuine kind of activism Watkins and others miss in the hip-hop "movement" really took hold in a national, cultural way, it would not be, by definition, a "hip-hop political agenda" at all. Watkins would likely imagine a different array of issues attended to than I would: my sense of real things happening to real people in the real America would not be based on being oppositional, and would not be the kind of thing that would be meaningfully symbolized by Eminem or P. Diddy or anyone else up on a stage walking back and forth yelling.

What's more, an underlying assumption of the hip-hop

"movement" idea is that the young voters we must bring to the polls will vote Democratic. This was, for example, the explicit goal in Russell Simmons's Rap the Vote effort in 2000. But even this has serious problems.

Informed black people are given to complaining that the Democrats take advantage of our vote—but insist on voting for them regardless, out of a sense that somehow, someday, black America will rise up and "demand" that their concerns be attended to. These days, Tavis Smiley's book *The Covenant* has sold like hotcakes in the black community, with each chapter on an issue relevant to black America including a boldface incantation "MOST OF ALL: Hold all leaders and elected officials responsible and demand that they change current policy."

It is unclear, however, just what this "demand" would consist of. Would it be with guns? I presume we're beyond that kind of thing. So how else? Well. Throughout history, if there's one thing we know, it's that stipulating that the Democrats will always get our vote whether or not they attend to our concerns is *not* the way to make change. That clearly makes no sense whatsoever.

There's something else we do know, which is that if the Democrats really had to work for our votes, they would be more moved to attend to black concerns. They would attend to black concerns if, when they did not, we, in significant numbers, took our vote elsewhere. That's how group politics has always worked. That's what a "demand" is about. What else would the demand be? Some black leader getting up and making a sonorous speech à la Reverend King? What would that speech consist of in 2008? "We *demand* . . . ,"

someone like maybe Tavis Smiley would say in this speech—
and aging white congressmen would start hammering out
new legislation, shaken to their cores by Smiley's "demand"?
What—are we going to riot again? The riots in Los Angeles
in 1992 have done nothing for anyone.

What would be behind the demand? We demand, or
else . . . what? That's what a demand is.

The Democrats should understand that blacks are different because we came here as slaves and that the demand
is upon their moral conscience? Well, *they don't understand.*
They understood it that way when the issue was something
as stark as Jim Crow and beating people up for trying to
vote. But beyond that, we all agree that they don't understand and show no signs of being about to. The Democrats,
in the real world of 2008, exploit the black vote, as we so
readily applaud when someone says it. What, then, is the
solution? Just "demanding" has not worked. We've tried
that, including to phat beats. It hasn't had any effect, and
thus we must move on.

Nor does it do a thing to register as an Independent as
a gesture of defiance against Democrats—but then keep on
voting for them, secure in your registered label implying
that you have a mind of your own and won't always vote
for them, even though you have, you do, and you will.

What *else* can we do? That is, to help people?

One tack would be to vote for the other party more often and leave Democrats in the lurch. Not always—or we'd
be right back where we are now. But despite the idea that it
is inauthentic for blacks to vote Republican, many Republican points are ones that are good for black people. No

Child Left Behind is not perfect, but it's better than what was going on before. Think about it: Republicans produced a bill that forces schools to pay attention to the race gap in scholastic achievement. Faith-Based Initiatives, funneling money to inner city churches and prisoner reentry programs, are good for black people, and supported by a great many black ministers. Or, many are under the impression that Latino immigrants depress wages for unskilled black Americans. The data do not really bear that out, but suppose you didn't know that: your view would be shared by Republicans, not Democrats. And so on. Maybe the Republicans' pro-black programs aren't perfect. But what Democratic programs are?

But I take the liberty of assuming that there won't be any hip-hop-led voter registration drives where attendees are educated about the value of Republican as well as Democratic programs to help black America. Hip-hop is about being confrontational, and that means Fighting the Powers That Be, and that is seen to be those evil, racist Republicans. Nas (who has stated to the media that he doesn't vote) reminded us on *Hip Hop Is Dead* that a black Republican is inherently a callous soul. So be it.

But that means that HSAN and its attendant ideology support a black voting pattern that leaves us America's least politically powerful minority group. Latinos and Asians split their vote much more evenly in the last presidential election—and note how so many Republicans have bent over backward lately in their voting patterns to avoid seeming against Latino immigrants. I find it hard to get excited about black voters rendering themselves irrelevant to that kind of attention, and even harder to get excited about a built-in idea that the black electorate is going to somehow "force" Democrats to "listen." That's one more way of talking about revolution, and there isn't going to be one. We fail ourselves with rhetoric of this kind.

Blood Diamonds

Who could fault Kanye West for presenting a revised version of his "Diamonds Are Forever" single on *Late Registration* in which he calls attention to the hideous conditions that African diamond miners work under? But there is, at present, a question as to whether this kind of consciousness raising can change anything. Is Kanye West's track changing the lives of the miners? So far, that has not happened. In any case, the question I am engaging in this book is whether hip-hop is going to spark a revolution in American politics on race. The diamonds issue is an African one. We should follow it, but it is not part of what I am addressing in this little book.

WHEN'S IT GONNA HAPPEN?

Something interesting about the Hip-hop Revolution is that, like the uprising of the proletariat that Marxists predicted, it seems to be ever in the future. We move ever further into the future in real life, but never any closer to that marvelous time when hip-hop becomes "a political tool" and starts improving lives.

It's been a while now. For example, the 1989 "Self

Destruction" video speaking against black-on-black violence is now a period piece, and the rate of homicides
among black teens remains appalling. It's been *a quarter of
a century* since writers first got excited about the "political
potential" of this music. It's not as if writers today excited
about hip-hop's "political potential" are referring to a music that emerged only ten years ago, not long enough to expect results just yet. Writers were depicting rap as possibly
sparking a political revolution *a quarter of a century ago*, in
the era of *Hill Street Blues*, Michael Jackson's *Thriller*, and
the Rubik's Cube; when VCRs were a new luxury item; the
media was abuzz with profiles of "yuppies" and "preppies";
e-mail, laptops, CDs, the Internet, and cell phones did not
exist; most people had never had sushi or Thai food; and
Madonna was the girl singing that new hit "Holiday." It's
been a long, long time. What's taking so long?

Think even about the "conscious" hip-hop tracks that
take a break from the fist-in-the-air posture and urge the
black community to look inward. Take, say, the "Skinz" track
on Pete Rock and C. L. Smooth's *Mecca and the Soul Brother*,
which one could justifiably have thought of as a positive
message in 1992. It urges black people to use condoms,
which would be especially germane nowadays with the AIDS
crisis in black communities. One may well have listened to
"Skinz" in 1992 and thought that maybe hip-hop of the
conscious kind might forge a revolution in black communities in terms of responsibility for sexual behavior.

The thing is, though, that 1992 was more than a
decade and a half ago. No revolution yet. Teen pregnancy
rates are down since then, yes, but it'd be hard to say that

"Skinz" or any of the other rap tracks addressing similar themes is the reason for that. And really, pregnancy rates are just down a tad, not enough to create any noticeable sea change in black communities where, obviously, women having babies as teenagers remains very common and perfectly ordinary. Dream now of hip-hop creating some kind of revolution, and consider that people had the exact same dream fifteen years ago—and started having it ten years before that.

Do we really have any reason to suppose that revolution is more likely to happen now than in 1992? Could it not be that this music is not, in the America we live in and know, going to create a revolution at all? Is the idea that hip-hop is "revolutionary" an actual engagement with reality, or is it, like so many of the routines in the music itself, such as the gunplay and recreational misogyny, a pose? Black America needs more than an attitude dressed up as an intention.

Das EFX's *Hold It Down* strikes me as having a certain quality that illustrates the reality of the "revolution" expectations about hip-hop. When this album was good, it was really good, such as in "Real Hip Hop" or "Here We Go." How can you resist an album where U-Haul, Maaco, RuPaul, and Jack Dempsey all pop up in one lyric?

Yet there are quite a few cuts on this album that sound a lot like the two I mentioned—the "crew" taking turns at the mike talking about how fierce they are. The rhymes are clever, but there is barely a time-out on the bragging, and after seventy-five minutes of it, it's hard not to miss that it's a pose. They were striking a pose to sell as "gangsta," as plenty of people before and after them had. After a while, an album like this sounds like a bunch of people saying, "Okay, here we go!" . . . but never going anywhere.

Example: cut number four was "Here We Go," while just two cuts later came "Here It Is." So apparently here we *went*, and now here it *was*. But where had we gone? And as to where they thought they were going, wasn't it just climbing to the heights of being really, really In Your Face? Let's take it that at "Here It Is," they reached that height—although "Here It Is" sounds no more In Your Face than "Here We Go." Never mind. What did the aforesaid height give anyone except something to move their bodies to?

Of course, Das EFX weren't presenting themselves as coffeehouse intellectuals. In "Hardcore Rap Act," we were told explicitly, "You never gonna catch me rappin' about no shit like the Government." But the running-in-place feel of that album feels to me exactly like the Hip-hop Revolution we are always being told is just over the horizon. There's a lot of noise, but nothing ever really happens.

Again, when will hip-hop go from potential to potent? I attended a conference back in 1998 at which the idea that hip-hop could become a political force was one of the main themes. Lots of smart black people were earnestly exploring that issue in talks and question sessions and snack break conversations—lots of talk of potential, focus. Every time a speaker uttered the word *hip-hop*, you could feel a little crackle in the room. But that crackle was based on the fact that hip-hop refers to good music that makes your body feel good because it has a nice beat, and the fact that hip-hop is an edgy voice from black people of humble circumstances, a voice which, to be sure, was heard from much less in the general American culture before hip-hop existed.

The assumption at the conference was that this voice was on its way to changing something, that it was a harbinger of something big finally happening, that this voice was just shy of being a vote, a political platform—a revolution.

But all I know is this: that was ten years ago, and yet the week you are reading this, there could be a conference where all of the exact same things are being said, with the exact same mood of hip-hop being *potentially* this, that, or the other. In fact, at some school somewhere in America there quite possibly either recently was or is about to be just such a conference.

But in the end, since 1998, hip-hop has shown no signs of moving anything. Or since 1993, when I met a young black guy on fire with the idea that his raps were going to "change thought" and help eradicate racism, and bitterly indignant at questions as to how that could possibly work. Or since 1982, when *Rolling Stone* went rhapsodic over Grandmaster Flash's "The Message" being significant as something beyond music. One aggrieved questioner at the conference I was at in 1998 even broke into reciting the "The Message" refrain "It's like a jungle sometimes . . . " The audience really liked that. "Here We Go," they felt— but now Here It Is, right where it started.

Isn't it time to let this whole notion go?

So many hold on to the idea that hip-hop is ever on the verge of lifting black America up in a political revolution. I am arguing that hip-hop is at heart all about acting up for its own sake. In evaluating which analysis is the right one, we might consider that while the "Hip-hop Revolution" is always and forever a possibility but never a reality, what hip-hop does create on a regular basis is high-profile battles between rappers. Some are rhetorical; some end up in violence and even murder. Yes, some of them are nurtured to help sell the music. But the fact is that these "beefs" are always around—and they are exactly what one would expect rap to create if its true soul is rhetorical testosterone wielded for thrills. A rapper gets killed somewhere almost once a month. Compared to this, any energy hip-hop has breathed into politics so far is a quiet little wheeze.

Cheryl Keyes says rap is "a powerful tool of dissuasion from social ills." But rap has never demonstrated anything of the sort. What makes Keyes characterize rap as powerful, I submit, is that it has a powerful *beat* and is a music of powerful *volume*. Keyes likes beat and volume. So do I, and so do all of us. Beat and volume, however, are not results. Or, they may result in a damned good time. That's a result, I guess. But it is not a *political* result.

"HOW COME WE AIN'T GETTIN' NO HIGHER?"
MAYBE IT'S JUST BEAUTIFUL MUSIC

"Music is supposed to inspire / How come we ain't gettin' no higher?" Lauryn Hill said on *The Miseducation of Lauryn Hill*. One reason is that "higher" is not endless variations on "whitey don't care about us." Higher is pointing us where to go despite the world not being perfect. I think that the musical warp and woof of hip-hop and its relentlessly alienated subtext are such that we cannot expect it be of much real help beyond making us feel good. The music, the beat, the atmosphere, the cultural associations are perfectly designed to rage and signify. In a way, it would have been more useful in 1960.

But today, the problems are different. One rages and rages, and nothing happens. The schools have plenty of money; it's what they do with it that is the problem—i.e., what *black* people do with it. Bringing edgy street cred to Albany does not take down laws. Rappers rage at registration rallies, but the fans moving to their beats do not then go out and vote for revolutionary candidates.

How many people listen to the latest Nas album and truly suppose—I mean, *honestly think*—that the raps on it, or any raps anywhere else, are going to stimulate more of what the old-time NAACP or Dr. King did? Elliott Wilson, black and working as an editor at the hip-hop magazine *XXL*, asked, "Who because of hip-hop now believes, 'I've seen the light, I'm going to save the blacks'?" We all know he's right.

I think Michael Eric Dyson knows what I mean. He writes of hip-hop that "its critics often fail to acknowledge that hip-hop is neither sociological commentary nor political criticism, though it may certainly function in these modes through its artists' lyrics." I'm not sure what this means, especially in a book devoting a whole chapter to hip-hop's political significance. It *isn't*, but it *might* be . . . ?! It might "function" as such. Why the careful remove of that Latinate word? Why not just *be* rather than "function"?

"Function" how? It seems as if Dyson is having it both ways—if hip-hop does "function" in a way that creates something, it's all good, but he's also got himself covered if it doesn't create anything, with his wording specifying that hip-hop is *not* commentary or criticism. That is, on some level he knows, as he openly said during a debate I did with him, that in the end hip-hop is just "all about the beat"—which in fact furnished the title of this book.

Hip-hop is all about the beat, but real world activism is *all about the work.*

The "Hip-Hop Revolution" idea implies that the work that's actually happening as I write is not the real deal, but a mere prelude to something that will only really take flight when hip-hop lifts it up with its pungent, take-no-prisoners street intensity.

There is, for example, a section of Bakari Kitwana's *The Hip Hop Generation* that I find odd in this way. He lists a number of people and organizations across America trying to make a difference for black people. However, his subtext is that all of this is just the stirrings of something more dramatic. Like almost all of the hip-hop intellectuals and chroniclers, Kitwana takes as a given that the Hip-Hop Revolution is a real possibility, that the black community should continue to urgently discuss it, and that academics and journalists should be grimly exploring just what this revolution ought to consist of and how to make it happen.

Kitwana is sincere, as are all of the people taking this revolutionary assumption as bedrock. But then, there is something that we might want to pay attention to amid all of this. We hear much about assorted organizations popping up here and there with the goal of forging political change through rap, rappers, and rebellious attitude. Some of them would include Conrad Muhammad's CHHANGE (Conscious Hip-Hop Activism Necessary for Global Empowerment), Chuck D's REACH (Rappers Educating All Curricula Through Hip-Hop), and the National Hip Hop Political Convention.

The people behind these organizations are doing their best, I'm sure. But truth to tell, have we really had any indication that these groups are getting anywhere? Don't they seem to be more a matter of perpetual anticipation? Frankly, try to get anywhere with the Web sites of outfits like these—if they even have them.

Sure, it's hard to get funding; it's hard to build an organization, much less keep it going. But—that's why with the ones that work, the key is a genuine mass energy behind the agenda, a wind beneath the wings. I do not mean any disrespect of the people involved in organizations like CHHANGE. But I submit: doesn't it look like the energy that would make these organizations real players is just not out there?

And is that really even a surprise? Since when does a political movement start with music and then add the activism? The Civil Rights Movement had the Freedom Songs, but at the beginning was the activism. At no point was anybody rushing around talking about how maybe the songs themselves might spark a movement.

Just imagine someone in 1949 saying, "These songs are great! They embody impatience with the status quo. 'We Shall Overcome,' 'Lift Ev'ry Voice and Sing'—let's take these songs and the feelings we have when we sing them and use them as a battering ram against Jim Crow!" No one said that, and thank God no one did. Or, if anyone did, we know nothing about it now, and shouldn't. The battering ram against Jim Crow was logic and hard work, implacable logic and bone-breaking, midnight-oil work—wielded by true activists like Charles Houston and Thurgood Marshall, leading to *Brown v. Board*; moral logic wielded by Dr. King from that jail in Birmingham. The hard organizational work by people like Bayard Rustin making the March on Washington happen and happen effectively.

But here we are today, listening to a music, thrilled by how it has emerged alongside some dress styles, body language, and attitudes, and thinking that this might translate into the hard work of political activism, grassroots organizing, and analyzing the system to find honest, realistic ways to make room for our concerns.

This is a plain example of trying to translate style into substance. Does anybody really think that something this bizarre could actually work just because Jay-Z and Common get up onstage and some people register to vote on their way out the door?

Make no mistake. Jay-Z and Common can make you feel really, really good. They can even make you think—gangsta Jay-Z as well as Common. But a political revolution?

I'm sorry. That idea may be many things. But one thing it is not is *real*.

CHAPTER FOUR

AIN'T LONG 'FORE YOU GET Y'ALL ACRES: HOW RADICAL POLITICS HOLDS BLACKS BACK

Tell 'em stay away from dem skyscrapers,
Ain't long 'fore you get y'all acres.

The Roots, "False Media," *Game Theory*

Years ago I attended a Saturday meeting of a local NAACP branch. The branch had fallen on hard times. Membership was down. The organization had little sway on the city's race scene, and they knew it. One of the heads of the organization was even committed to curbing a tendency for some members to sermonize at great length rather than work on concrete solutions to the city's problems.

The attendees comprised two groups. One was the old heads—people seventy and older who had been members since before the Civil Rights revolution, courtly, bespectacled folk in suits and dresses, quietly distressed and perplexed as to why black people in the city were in such a bad way after so much opportunity had opened up.

The other group, larger, was modern black folks, with

more "flava" than the older ones, grimly indignant. All were given to lengthy, sonorous speeches about (1) how black people needed to raise their kids better and (2) how black people are still struggling under the white man's foot on their necks.

It was a meeting of speeches. The organizers were hoping it would be a meeting about action, but all morning, speeches were the main meal. You could tell that meetings of this NAACP branch had been all about these same speeches year after year for a very long time. The meetings had been about performances: individuals wielding ringing phraseology, showing that they were hip to a "conscious" gospel, and more interested in doing that than translating that hipness into action, activism. Activism would have meant letting go of the easy self-medication of versifying about how things aren't right. Activism would have meant stepping outside of what medicated the self and getting down to actually doing the work.

The meeting was supposed to go from nine to five. However, that same afternoon, black ministers in the city were doing a march on a local issue of the moment couched in a "Fight the Power" orientation. Throughout the morning there loomed a question as to whether after lunch, the members were going to go march with the ministers (for the local news cameras) or stay in the conference room (bland and windowless, with no cameras or drama) and hammer out a plan for serious activism, distinct from the treading water that had been the lay of the land for the branch for too long.

The question was, then, whether to strike a pose against whitey or do the mundane but crucial work of figuring out how to help people in an era when blame is assignable in many directions. The majority that ruled went with their gut—they got out into the street to make noise. At one P.M., most of the members left to participate in that march. The meeting was over. It had been three hours of noble speechifying instead of seven hours of creating something. An NAACP branch in, say, 1950 would have found seven hours of creating something normal. To this branch that afternoon, such a seven hours would have felt, one could not help but sense, boring.

So much for the afternoon session of working out a game plan that would connect this NAACP to the city's black population in a real way. So much for these people following in the footsteps of Reverend King and his associates, who hammered out detailed and concrete plans for black advancement and haggled over them with the Powers That Were. This aspect of what the SCLC did was not recorded on film to be replayed and stir us like King's "I Have a Dream" speech, but this brass-tacks engagement with detail was more central to creating opportunity for blacks than the speech alone, or any other speech King or anyone else made.

These modern NAACP members did not understand that. What they knew was gesture, posture, gut, heat, picture, turning it out.

Praise their "passion." But today, unlike the March on Washington, the ministers' march that afternoon had no historical resonance—in the local newspapers it made barely a blip. The only people who remember it today were either in it or happened to be there when it went by. It had no effect on the lives of black folks in that city, where today rising murder rates and feeble public schools remain as much in the headlines as they were then. It was merely that day's gesture, attitude, drama.

To this day, that NAACP branch remains as irrelevant to the lives of its supposed flock as it was years ago. Last I heard, its new president was planning a youth center and a program to teach young blacks more black history. Very 1972, and like countless initiatives of that kind since then, it will change nothing.

The politics of hip-hop are the politics of the younger contingent at that NAACP meeting, giving performance pride of place over engaging with the complexities of our moment. The idea is that just as charismatic protest gained us so much in the 1950s and 1960s, street performances today will gain us more. If we just keep at it, something seismic will happen again, supposedly.

But even the Civil Rights revolution took *350 years* to happen, and when it finally did, it was the result of a chance confluence of historical circumstances. Those are now long in the past, and the future of black America will be about gradual, less dramatic kinds of change—not because I want it to be that way, but because there is no logical way that it could be otherwise.

I feel it important to spell out why I believe this is true, because to embrace an idea that a new revolution is coming, from hip-hop or anywhere else, is to divert energy that would be better directed to truly progressive efforts. The dramatic appeal of the revolutionary idea is obvious, but in this case, it's a distraction, and a dangerous one. There is work to be done out there, and too many of our discussions float above it.

"WE MET—THEREFORE WE WON!"

While we're on 1972, as a matter of fact, let's take a trip back in time.

The radical fist-in-the-air version of black politics did not start with Public Enemy, after all. Black people have been embracing this way of looking at things for forty years now. Crucially, this version of politics has had no serious results.

Let's take a look back to what in 1972 was considered a big deal on the black scene, the National Black Political Convention in Gary, Indiana. It was thought to imprint the militant Black Power ideology as mainstream, and in an emblematic sense, it did. From then on, the assumption took hold that being really black was being really mad *whether or not the madness led to anything.*

This thing was in all the papers and magazines. There was a documentary. This was the Million Man March of the era—and ended up having the exact same effect on black lives afterward: none.

All the elements we now associate with "real black" positions were on view. There was the idea that black America was ever poised to rise up in a revolutionary way that would transform the nation, such that the Long,

Hot Summers of burning down our own neighborhoods were mere rehearsals of something bigger to come. Jesse Jackson, with a big afro, sang that "The water has broke. The blood is spilled. A new black baby is going to be born."

There was the DuBois fetish, when Gary's mayor Richard Hatcher, a black man, summoned his spirit. Here was the conviction that DuBois, with his grim message about black people having achingly bifocal identities torn between the white and the black, and this meaning that black people were America's main problem, was the soul of blackness. More to the point, here was the idea that every black individual carries a special badge as a standing indictment of America's eternal racism. To be black is to be a uniquely fraught person serving to remind white people of their nation's original sin, demanding ritual and even cyclical (Black History Month?) expiation, on NPR and beyond.

You had your black nationalism, with the "Republic of New Africa" contingent proposing that five Black Belt states secede as a separate nation. Reparations were discussed long before Randall Robinson's hit book *The Debt*. The convention included "Queen Mother" Audley Moore (note the African feel of the "Queen") angry that slavery deprived her of a "pretty black color." And outside the convention hall a guy was going around with a plaque on his body saying that Jesus was black.

Plus, there were already notions now familiar from rap "politics." There was the idea that the speaker calling and the audience responding was a herald to action: Jesse Jackson hollered, "When we form our own political party what time is it?" and the audience hollered back, "Nation Time!" There was the idea that hollering alone was constructive. Thomas Fortune, assemblyman from Brooklyn, exclaimed afterward, "We met—therefore we won!" Won what? It must have sounded great when he said it, but what did we "win" just by convening in one place? That's political activism? Not of a kind that Susan B. Anthony, Emma Goldman, Che Guevara, César Chávez, or even Dr. King would have recognized.

There was even the swooning over tart musical texture as politically important, with one journalist noting the "gutsy" tone of the music in the air, and the "force and undercurrent of driving drums"—exactly the sort of thing that would elate people as politically meaningful in rap music in the next decade.

And Amiri Baraka was there.

All of this could have happened last week. You could put a concerned black person of today in the audience at this convention in 1972, and the only things they would find different from innumerable conferences, assemblies, forums, panel discussions, and community meetings on black issues since then up to last Friday would be that in 1972 almost nobody was talking about affirmative action, and there wasn't yet a pantheon of numerous blacks in very high places like Condoleezza Rice, Colin Powell, Oprah Winfrey, Richard Parsons, and Tiger Woods to dismiss as traitors or accidents. The National Black Political

Convention set the terms of a conversation that we have been having over and over again ever since.

And for what?

"A new black baby is going to be born." Well, in fact a great many were born after that, too many, in the opinion of almost everyone, especially in poor black neighborhoods where most of the people having such babies would have been better advised to have many fewer. Or, to address what Jackson said on the metaphorical level, since 1972, what "black baby" has been born kicking The Man's ass? Last time I checked, the going wisdom was that black people are still stunted by the likes of institutional racism. Say that black America has made significant gains since 1972 and you are smacked down by people insisting that this has only been among middle-class blacks. To these people, middle-class blacks do not qualify as a black baby being born, but as beside the point, of questionable classification as "real" black people anyway, since they opt not to reside in the 'hood.

As to black nationalism, the notion that there will ever be an actual physical black American nation is long dead on the vine. Meanwhile, reparations got a lot of attention for a few years after 2000, but these days, its advocates have given up on the fantasy that white America will get on its knees and apologize for slavery and Jim Crow with cash disbursements of any kind. Instead, by all indications as I write, some big companies just might cough up some money to atone for having benefitted from the slave trade centuries ago, and whatever comes of that will have no significant impact on the lives of black people on real-life streets.

Or: "We met—therefore we won!" With sincere regret, and equally sincere respect for people at this convention who were genuinely aroused by the new mood, I must ask: What did you win?

Imagine a black history chronicle written in 2050, with an entry for the National Black Political Convention of 1972. Now: what benefits to black America would this encyclopedia entry list as having been fostered by that convention? What change, what policy, happened as the result of that convention that helped black people who needed help? The answer is: none.

However stirring the speeches were, however excited people were afterward for a week or three, the National Black Political Convention created not a single thing. It led to no political party. It had no effect on the evolution of policy in Washington. In fact, underneath the celebratory veneer, there had been more than a little bit of disagreement, as assorted factions, although supposedly all "representing black people," had a hard time finding common ground.

In retrospect, despite what people there were hoping it would be, in terms of its effect upon later events, it was simply an event, a gathering, a party. It created nothing.

And wouldn't you know—that party, despite not having accomplished anything, has inspired a splinter group seeking a "Hip-Hop Revolution," the National Hip Hop Political Convention.

THE CIVIL RIGHTS REVOLUTION:
WHAT WAS SPECIAL ABOUT JUST THEN?

It's important to remember the National Black Political Convention, because it is exactly this kind of event, this kind of rhetoric, and this kind of atmosphere that people hoping for a Hip-Hop Revolution have in mind. People are under an impression that black people speaking angrily and dramatically, making frequent references to racism and rebirth, with rhythmic music playing in the background and some media coverage, is in some fashion a political action of significance, the beginning of something larger.

But it isn't always. It can end up just being a show. In fact, I would say that it usually is.

The March on Washington and other events were indeed the spark for something larger. But in the light of day, we have to stop and consider what is really going on in America and in the world today. Look at the headlines in today's newspaper, or watch CNN for a half hour. Then think about what's been in the paper and on the news over, say, the past ten years, and if you're inclined, think about what will likely be in the news next year and the year after that. Can you honestly say that you glean the slightest sign that there is going to be a repeat of the Civil Rights revolution?

Remember that even the Million Man March in 1996 was supposed to be something along those lines—and look at the result. Okay, some people *registered* to vote, but see the previous chapter about the difference between registering to vote and actually voting. Are black people now voting in some fashion sparked by the Million Man March? No. In fact, more black voters describe themselves as Independent now than they did in 1996—i.e., fewer blacks describe themselves as exclusively Democratic, which is the way the Million Man March presumed its flock would vote. If the Million Man March had seeded a revolution in thought and commitment, then presumably there wouldn't be people a dozen years later hoping there would be a "Hip-Hop Revolution" in voting patterns.

"As a result of the Million Man March, black America now, in contrast to before the march, _____." Try filling in that blank. It's just, well, a blank. The Million Man March yielded a lasting image of lots of black men in one place, and a nice movie by Spike Lee. However, it changed not a single thing. That kind of drama cannot change anything in our era.

We're at war, in more than one place. The main issues on the nation's mind are the financial instability of the middle class, the mess of our health care system, how to manage immigration, the state of our schools, and global warming. This is not a time when it seems at all plausible that the concerns of a certain segment of a single minority group out of many will be embraced by the nation as a top concern. The issues most discussed intersect with race here and there (especially schools), but the era of the White House committing itself in a sustained way to the specific task of uplifting black people is far in the past.

Think of the most influential movie documentaries to-day: *Fahrenheit 9/11*, on the Iraq War; *An Inconvenient Truth*, on global warming. On black issues, the hot ones are questioning the leftist take, not shoring it up. Byron Hurt may open his *Hip-Hop: Beyond Beats and Rhymes* by getting in "I love hip-hop," but the documentary is all about questioning hip-hop's core attitudes. Janks Morton's *What Black Men Think* is in a similar vein, questioning the idea that "ghetto" is the best track for black men. The old-school rhetoric of black revolution is just that—old school.

That sounds pessimistic, I know. It seems as if I am missing that things often looked just as hopeless to Civil Rights leaders in the past, but that they had faith. However, I am not being pessimistic: I am being logical. Civil Rights leaders had had faith since the early nineteenth century, but had to be satisfied with a mix of brutal setbacks (*Plessy v. Ferguson*) and incremental gains (A. Philip Randolph getting Franklin D. Roosevelt to institute the Fair Employment Practices Committee policing discrimination against blacks in the defense industry and government jobs in 1941).

The Civil Rights leaders in the fifties and sixties managed to give us so much not just because they had faith. Frederick Douglass had had faith a hundred years earlier. The Civil Rights revolution happened when it did because of the combined effect of three chance developments.

First, President John F. Kennedy and Attorney General Robert Kennedy had a special interest in race issues because the virtual apartheid in America posed a public relations problem amid our Cold War with Russia. It was awkward to condemn the Communist way of life while black people were getting beaten in the streets on the front pages of the newspapers. Both Kennedys were otherwise very much of their time, neither having the ingrained sense that to be racist is morally equivalent to being a pedophile, so common a notion in much of white America in our times. It is sobering, for example, to see how little interest Franklin Roosevelt, even with his relentless commitment to the redistributionist framework of the New Deal, had in black people. The New Deal was about poor people, not "Negroes" specifically. Minus the Cold War, the Kennedy brothers would likely have been little more interested in the black condition than Roosevelt was. It is possible that there would have been no developments as decisive as the Civil Rights Act and the Voting Rights Act.

Second, the Civil Rights revolution happened within a historical window, 1924 to 1965, when there was much less immigration into the United States than there had been before. The Immigration Act of 1924 limited immigration from any country to 2 percent of the number of people from that country who had been in the United States in 1890. Asians were barred altogether. As a result, there was much more of a space in the public consciousness for black people to attract and hold on to attention. In 1940, for instance, there were fewer than 2 million Latinos in America, as opposed to 13 million blacks.

However, right after the Civil Rights and Voting Rights Acts, the Immigration Act of 1965 opened the gates to immigrants once again. This created the multicultural America we know and love today, but it also means that black concerns now compete with those of Asians, Latinos, actual Africans, and so many others. Blacks and Latinos in the United States today are roughly tied in number, at about 35 million. The question arises as to what would unify public sentiment now behind the concerns of black people alone.

Some would answer that we have pride of place because our ancestors were brought here as slaves and then endured Jim Crow. It is rather plain in 2008, however, that this *moral* (rather than logical) argument does not arouse many people anymore. The general sentiment is that the Civil Rights revolution itself, plus affirmative action, scholarships, monuments, and holidays, have been acknowledgment enough.

Our concern is what works, not what makes for stirring rhetoric. Arguing that black people merit special attention because of our special history may be plausible to many black people and some white ones, but in 2008, it no longer *works* with the American public in general—and after the stirring rhetoric, we are stuck forever with the American public. The case has become too abstract. Most people are not historians. In the sixties, we were fighting present-day Jim Crow. Today, we make a case based on what happened eons ago and its "legacy" and so forth. That argument is too "deep" to resonate significantly with the American polity.

Those arguing that black people are a special case readily agree that America does not "hear" them. They must now admit that they can present no way that this would change—which will require facing up to the fact that rallies where rappers "represent" don't seem to be making a difference, any more than anything else has over the past forty years. The "conscious" response after this is to engage in real activist efforts seeking to go forward *despite* the fact that Joe Barstool and Joe Congressman will never feel as culpable as we might wish.

Say that rap "could" change Joe's mind—and answer as to how far rap has gotten in doing so in thirty years. Also, explain how things are different now, such that some *more* rap will finally make Joe wake up. Just what is it about today's rap that looks like it will finally do the job?

Finally, part of why black concerns gained a place in the public conversation in the sixties was that television was a novelty. For the first time, white people actually watched the barbarities of Jim Crow happening vividly on news film in their living rooms, rather than just seeing photographs in the paper. It is possible that if television had come along in 1910, then lynching would have ended sooner, for example. However, televised moving and speaking images of the results of injustice are not a novelty today, and never can be again. Or, when now and then an image of this kind does strike a chord, such as the Rodney King video, the response it creates is of ambiguous long-term value, because the issues today are more complex than the issues of fifty years ago. After the verdict in favor of the officers who beat King, young black men burned down their own neighborhoods, and today, no one could

point to anything constructive that resulted from their doing so. There is no indication of a "revolution" of any kind
in what resulted from the Rodney King episode or any others like it since.

Thus, despite all of the passion and faith that earlier
black leaders like W. E. B. DuBois and Ida B. Wells had a
hundred years ago, history was not on their side the way it
was for Martin Luther King. There was something particular about America in the two decades after World War II. In
fact, part of what makes Civil Rights leaders of this era so
awe-inspiring is that they had little way of knowing that
history was on their side. They changed things step by step,
often despairing that no further steps would ever work out,
and saw the most massive revolution in a nation's racial
consciousness in human history.

But the fact remains: they were borne on the tide of a
coincidence of historical factors, difficult for any individual
living day to day to perceive the import of, but decisive all
the same. Civil Rights leaders just as committed in 1890
saw no such victories because the stars weren't aligned the
way they would happen to be seventy years later. There's a
reason a name like William Monroe Trotter has little resonance today. When people like this were on fire, white
America wasn't interested in them yet.

Today, in a way, we are in 1920. History is not on the
side of revolution now. If anyone can name three or four
aspects of our times that could lead to a second revolution
targeted for black people specifically, right now, in the
America that we live in today, then I bow down to
them. But it'd be a tough business to come up with

things that give serious indication of being relevant. What about our times right now leads you to think that America could turn upside down again regarding black people? I don't mean in a sense that involves going into a dreamy, preaching mode. I mean in the concrete sense, here, now, based on what you read in the paper. Can you honestly say that you can imagine another revolution of any kind on race evolving from our America right now as you know it?

For one thing, notice that the racial group getting real attention these days is not black people but Latinos. They have a massive influence on policy; namely, immigration policy, because their views on how illegal immigrants are treated in this country are deeply held and determine much of their voting patterns. There is no equivalent issue for black people today. The attention race gets these days in terms of monthly dustups over hate speech has nothing to do with legislation giving real uplift to black people who need it.

Even with his theme of populist outrage, John Edwards did not propose that any black man not on his way to college will have a factory job available a bus ride away. Edwards could never promise that, because America has changed, in a way that cannot be reversed, because this is a capitalist country and people in China work more cheaply than American factory workers would. Edwards did not propose that America go socialist, and Edwards was not all about black people.

I know what some are thinking: suppose Barack Obama gets to the White House. Well, he shows no affinity toward creating a black revolution either, black though he is. Remember, Obama is all about bringing the nation together, not turning it upside down. He's no black radical and makes sure we know it. Other younger black politicians who have reached the national public eye are of similar orientation these days. Harold Ford, Jr., Artur Davis, and Deval Patrick are not about "getting up on some real shit on Capitol Hill." They care about black people, but they are also insiders.

WHAT WOULD A REVOLUTION CALL FOR?

A question that must be asked is also just what a black revolution would even be about today. Certainly black America has serious problems. However, a revolution does not consist solely of howling grievances. For a revolutionary effort to be worth anyone's time, the demands have to be ones that those being revolted against have some way of fulfilling.

In one episode of the animated version of Aaron McGruder's *The Boondocks*, there is an articulate depiction of the idea that black people need to Rise Up as a group and Make Demands. Huey, whose bitter frown is as ingrained in his design as a vapid smile is on Mickey Mouse, imagines that Martin Luther King comes back to life and inspires a revolution in black America, graphically indicated as hordes of blacks swarming the gates at the White House. "It's fun to dream," Huey concludes, the idea being that black people know what to rise up against, but that they would run up against the heartless moral cesspool that is AmeriKKKa, where, say, "George Bush doesn't care about black people."

But the question is: what would the people at the gates, if attended to, demand? Fifty years ago, the demands were obvious: dismantle Jim Crow. And since then, a lot more has been given: affirmative action, the transformation of welfare from a stingy program for widows to an open-ended dole for any unmarried woman with children (done largely as riot insurance in the late 1960s, called for by left-ist activists including black ones) . . . I could go on.

So—yes, black America still has problems. Yes, there is still racism. But what is it that the White House should do now, in 2008, that is staring everyone in the face but hasn't happened because white people just "don't care" and the black community has failed to "demand" it? What? Precisely?

I am not implying that what needs to happen is black people getting acquainted with those "bootstraps" we hear so much about. But the problems are not the kind that could be solved by simply buckshotting whitey with the usual cries of "racism."

Would the people at the gates be calling for inner city schools to get as much money as schools in leafy white suburbs? If they did, they would see the same thing that has happened when exactly that was done in places like New Jersey and Kansas City: nothing changes. Obviously something needs to be done about the schools. But what, of the sort that should be shouted through the White House fence? How many of the shouters would know about poor black kids kicking academic butt in KIPP schools? Or in other charter schools filled with kids there because of—oh dear—vouchers, in Ohio and Florida? Let's face it—most of the people at that fence would draw a blank on what KIPP schools even were, much less the good that vouchers are doing. Some revolution.

Would the people at the gates be calling for police forces to stop beating up on young black men and sometimes killing them? Well, that's a legitimate concern. But the revolution on that is already happening, in every American city making concerted efforts to foster dialogue between the police and the street. We're not there yet, but things are better. Anyone who says that the shooting death of Sean Bell in 2006 in New York was evidence that nothing had changed since the death of Amadou Diallo in 1998 knows little of what the relationship between the police and black people was like in New York and so many other places before the nineties. In 1960, the death of Amadou Diallo would have made the local papers only, for one day, and, even in those papers, on some back page. It wouldn't have been considered important news. Going through newspapers of that era, one constantly comes across stories about things that happened to "Negroes," on page A31, that today would be front-page breaking news. We are blissfully past that America.

And back to the main point: what could the White House do to prevent things like the Diallo and Bell incidents? What simple, wave-the-wand policy point would make it so that never again would a young black man be killed by the police in dicey circumstances where every-body lost his head for a minute or so? The relationship between police forces and black people is not as simple as something that could be changed by storming through a gate, which is obvious from how persistent that prob-lem has been despite profound changes on so many other fronts.

Would the people at the gates be calling for employers to stop being less interested in applications from people with names like Jamal and Tamika than in those from Justin and Megan? Again, how could a fiat from the White House change that? After all, the study that showed this tendency—these days often brought forth as evidence that racism is still a defining experience of being black—did not show that the Jamals and Tamikas in question do not get jobs anyway. That study did not show that contrary to our experience it is still 1956. It showed that there are still certain backward people, certain biases—but not ones re-motely powerful enough to leave Jamal or Tamika on the unemployment line. If Jamal and Tamika were barred from *all* or even *most* career-level employment because of their names, then there would be grounds for requiring the White House, Congress, or the Supreme Court to step in. But instead, Jamal and Tamika get jobs, just not at the oc-casional firm where whites happen to get a little worried about names like that.

So, yes, there is "some racism"—but how could a president change that? What would the president do? How could the president change the gut feelings of people he doesn't even know? How could the president change the gut feelings of, really, anyone? What would the revolutionaries at the fence seek to do for Jamal and Tamika?

Another thing making black issues too complex and abstract to stimulate a coherent uprising is that as the result of the freedoms given by the Civil Rights revolution, there is not, in a true sense, a single "black community" anymore. There was a time when even the most educated, wealthy blacks were firmly barred from high positions in American life. Naturally, then, there was a defined sense of blacks being a single community, especially given that in so many cities, even accomplished, affluent blacks could only reside in black sections of town.

Those days are past. Even if successful blacks encounter some racism in their lives, in 2008 racism alone does not define how most black human beings sense their existences, despite what many academics seem to want us to think. The overall life experiences of an affluent black person and a working-class one are different enough today that our sense of a black community is much more fluid and abstract—and the fact that affluent blacks get pulled over on drug checks now and then does not change that.

A revolution would need a more urgent sense of community. Glenn Loury puts this well, describing the old-time black community as

> geographically concentrated in the South of the United States; that was culturally homogenous; that had institutions because of the requirements

and the necessity of their separation. They were segregated. It was a necessity to create institutions. Of course they educated their own children. Who else would do it?

What we speak about now are cities with hundreds of thousands of people mired in a dead end. It is not a community. It does not have an articulated social structure of middle-class and upper-class people and educated workers and carpenters and all the rest living together in harmony. The civil society, the mediating institutions, are thin.

HIP-HOP MESSAGE OR PROGRESSIVE MESSAGE?

The "message" of hip-hop can be fairly described as saying two things. The first one: "Things really suck." The second: "Things will keep sucking until there is a revolution where the white man finally understands and does a complete 180-degree turn."

I see this as a message of weakness and passivity. I see it that way for a very specific reason: there is no logical way that the revolution in question could ever happen. It may be fun to think about, but in the light of day, it is nothing but an idle fantasy. The sixties will not happen again.

I say that not because I have some problem with how our Civil Rights heroes made the sixties happen. I say that not because I have some reserved, bourgeois antipathy toward noise. I am not saying that protest is inappropriate. I am saying that the call to turn the system upside down was useful and bore fruit in the fifties and sixties as the result of a chance confluence of several factors that could never occur again. I stress: *it was useful and it bore fruit.* I fully understand my debt to my elders. It was useful and it bore fruit—*then.* But now is not then.

I am saying that today, the call to turn the system up-side down is not effective in addressing the problems we face in our own era, and when wielded, it does little but provide for street theater without actually helping anyone. The problems are different. Real solutions will go far be-yond telling white people to stop doing something. Once again: *that indeed was the kind of solution that worked in the fifties and sixties.* But now it is not.

And for that reason, I believe that politics regarding black America that can be classified as revolutionary, radi-cal, or nationalist disregard the very people those politics claim to be concerned about. Rap of a "revolution," of we "niggas" rising up from a cage, and you are preaching a message of defeat, stasis, impotence—because what you are really saying is that black America will only improve when whites again change the way they think. We all know none of that shows any sign of ever happening. It appeals merely in the artistic sense. Rapping "Things suck" and leaving it there is not prophetic but weak. Wack, I might say.

It's like someone singing "Twinkle, twinkle, little star" . . . and then just sitting there, as you ache to hear them complete it with "How I wonder what you are." Or, more apropos, imagine Jay-Z on *Reasonable Doubt* yelling "Can I kick it?" and the track just ending there. Obviously, what's supposed to come next is "Yes, you can!!!!" In other words, on inequality, can we kick it? Yes, we can—if we get back to real civil rights and start fetishizing solutions rather than postures. We get nowhere in thinking that to be political is just to, as it were, "kick it," in the sense of making noise, enjoying the idle self-medication of being angry. Jay-Z accusing the Bush administration of racism in "Minority Report" is one thing, but it is still a static gesture. He's saying: *shit!* I seek more than this in something presented to me as politically significant.

In 2008, all indications are that black America is going to overcome rather quietly. Definitely but quietly. "Ain't long for you get y'all acres," Black Thought tells us, the subtext being that just over the horizon, blacks will finally get that forty acres and a mule. But no, it's not going to go down that way, not with that brand of drama. Some will never be able to muster much interest in change that happens quietly, gradually—or even definitively. Change it may be, but not interesting. Not worthy of writing articles about. Not worthy of mentioning at book signings. Not *the shit*. This is because they are wedded to a fantastical notion that change will happen in a way that starkly gets back at "whiteness" and occurs to the kind of beat that gets them moving in their seats.

These people are, in the end, pleasing themselves rather than thinking seriously about how the nation operates and how to carve a space within it where black people who need help can get it. Those of us interested in helping people— which is different from utopian leftist incantations—must walk on by. What really helps people? Frankly, it has no beat. You can't dance to it. It isn't in anyone's face. It is, in a word—a word used in an original sense that hip-hop has distracted us from—*real*.

REASONS FOR HOPE

Snapping our necks to beats and rhymes will have no effect on what happens in the congressional chamber.

But all is not lost. Unlike in 1920, we have the advantage that the Civil Rights revolution did happen forty years ago, and mainstream attitudes in America did change. They did not change in such a way as to be interested in a black Civil Rights revolution occurring *again*. But as the result of awareness of the first one, philanthropists are wide open to funding efforts targeted at poor black people. Grassroots organizations like the Harlem Children's Zone are supported in part by rich white people, after all. Corporations are behind organizations like this in any city: in Indianapolis, Christamore House, helping turn lives around in the inner city, is backed by Eli Lilly. In 1920, to most people with money, black uplift efforts sounded about as important as saving spotted owls.

Washington may not be set to apply a Marshall Plan to black ghettoes—and it's not an easy question as to just where the funds would go under such a plan (e.g., recall that flooding bad schools with money results in well-funded bad schools). However, Washington does create programs like No Child Left Behind, the Faith-Based Initiatives, the Second Chance Act reintegrating ex-cons into society, and the Responsible Fatherhood and Healthy Families Act. There are flaws in all of them. But in 1920 all of them would have sounded like something from the fourth dimension. As they would have as late as 1990. As late as *2000*, efforts that have now culminated in the Second Chance Act were seen as rewarding the "undeserving poor."

We have something to work with today. Of course racism is still around. But in deciding what is possible today, black people must do their grandparents the courtesy of remembering what America was like in the old days. In this, black people will also do themselves a courtesy, in working from what is constructive and positive about our times. Smoking out one more indication that racism is still alive in subliminal ways must be less interesting to us than coping, dealing, building. If black people did this when they weren't even allowed to eat with white people in public, then surely we can do this now. Pretend that black people need the total eclipse of racism to do anything better than okay, and you are disappointing the spirits of our elders.

Michael Eric Dyson in his *Holler If You Hear Me* seems especially taken with Tupac's line "I'm hopeless." Dyson enshrines that line as a message to white America to "save" this hopeless person with, by implication, a radical recasting of how America works. But for forty years America has shown no sign of heeding that message in the way that people like Dyson intend. Rather, there are efforts across the nation addressing that hopelessness in ways that are quiet, incremental—and effective. What justifies treating those things as beside the point, and instead chanting eternally that some Great Awakening is what truly wise, moral people must attend to?

Is the reason that the Great Awakening idea sits well on a beat?

I suspect no one will respond, "Yes, I prefer politics that sit well on a beat." But with all due respect, I think that deep down, the seduction of rhythm is indeed much of why so many people entertain the prospect of a revolution based on rap music. Let's look at that issue.

CHAPTER FIVE

MOVING YOUR BODY WHILE SITTING IN YOUR SEAT: IS RHYTHM TRUTH?

*Ya start poppin' your fingers and stompin' ya feet,
and movin' your body while you're sittin' in your seat.*

"Rapper's Delight"

Entertaining the idea of rap being a political force is, well, entertaining. Yet I think almost anyone understands deep down that it's a queer notion in the end. There is, at this point, a certain vocabulary and phraseology that the "Hip-Hop Revolution" idea is couched in, with a tacit agreement not to ask too many questions about feasibility.

Actually listen to a rap track, even by a conscious artist, and then think about the real world. How many among us really believe there is a meaningful connection between that rap and making people think in new ways—ways so new that the nation's fabric changes?

Claims that hip-hop is more than music is what George Orwell termed "gumming together long strips of words which have already been set in order by someone else, and making the results presentable by sheer humbug."

That must be clear to pretty much everybody on some level. However, there is apparently something about hip-hop that distracts people into, in some part of their brains, seeing something in it that is, as Young Jeezy has it in his album title, inspirational.

From what I see, it's the beat.

Talking to people about hip-hop, watching people talk about it, overhearing people talk about it, one sees that people hear a certain truth in a statement when it is uttered over a beat. The rhythm is regular, and in the mind, the sense of regularity spills over into how we perceive the meaning of the sentence. Rhythm is deeply seductive. Even babies like it. It is so seductive that it can discourage reflection, and in the case of the idea of rap as politically significant, I think it is doing precisely that.

WHAT HE SAID VERSUS HOW HE SAID IT

This is a delicate point because it touches on an aspect of black culture traditionally celebrated as one of its crowning "diversities"—the call-and-response tradition. But the power of this new music is so distracting that this is a time when we must "go there." As I once heard Stanley Crouch put it, at a time when I thought the topic was taboo, black people need to get beyond the idea that something is true just because it is expressed in infectious rhythm. I would add that any white rap fans under a similar impression need to get beyond it as well.

When a black speaker begins an address to a black group or congregation with "Good afternoon" and the room responds in unison, "Good afternoon," who would have a problem with that? It's warm, it traces to Africa. Fine. Also fine is that part of the effectiveness of a black (or fundamentalist) church sermon is the rhythmic cadence of the sentences, punctuated by people's "Amens" and other responses.

But too often in the black community this way of listening drifts into an unspoken idea that rhythm and inflection are meaning in itself.

I once attended a talk by a black academic who decorated his points with lines from old blues songs. Every time he chanted one of these lines, a good portion of the black people in the audience would *mm-hmm* warmly. However, the average age of the audience tilted young. Most were in their twenties and thirties, and yet many of them were doing the *mm-hmms* even when the man was quoting antique or obscure blues lines that people their age were unlikely to be familiar with. Most of them were almost certainly more familiar with hip-hop and R&B than with Robert Johnson and Blind Lemon Jefferson.

What warmed them was the sheer cadence of the man's utterance of the lines. Each time he quoted a line, it was like bringing the audience to church for a few seconds. He went over well—but the truth was that, that night at least, he never actually said much of anything. But to many of the blacks in the audience, the *feel* of what he said *was* what he said. If what he actually uttered were written out on paper, where melody and rhythm could not come through, no one would think much of it at all.

I imagine that assorted academics and artists might

sincerely embrace the idea that there are implications hidden behind and swirling around words and sentences that on the surface seem to have only mundane, concrete meanings. But this kind of thing, implying that truth is a matter of something that one merely "feels"—eyes closed, harkening to the "vibe" (e.g., "Ya feel me?")—is too vague and personal to have anything to do with politics that help real people here in the real world.

When it comes to how a black professor goes over in a bookstore talk about literature one night, processing texture as meaning does no harm. The problem is when we start pretending that rhythms and inflections—color, we might say—constitute coherent political insight worthy of extended attention. People who think hip-hop is politics are falling for the visceral sense that beat, pulse, feel, is meaning, and in a "realer" way even than words, sentences, logical connections, genuinely "conscious" thought.

This will not do when generations of black people's lives are at stake. It must be resisted. We cannot revert to ways of thinking typical of unlettered tribespeople when grappling with what ails black people this week in Cleveland. Words, sentences, logical connections, and constructive thought will be our salvation. Mysticism will not—even if it's set to a great rhythm track.

Ralph Ellison was hip to this, once complaining during the Black Power era, "Just give the most banal statement a rhyme and a rhythm, put a little strut into it, and we'll grab it like a catfish gulping down a piece of dough-bait."

A graphic indication of how unrelated truth can be to

rhythm is a now classic image promulgated on the black comedy circuit, sadly reflecting a reality: the black woman in a club happily dancing with her hands in the air to raps calling black women bitches and ho's. The women in question are given to saying, "I know he's not talking about me," but, as we all know, he is. *Bitch* and *ho* in this music do not, as Snoop Dogg once implied in a press interview, refer only to a particular sort of low-rent "golddigger" kind of person (although that would be mean enough). Maybe that's what Snoop Dogg meant fifteen years ago on an album like *Doggystyle*, but on countless hip-hop tracks since then, *bitch* and *ho* refer not to a particular type of woman, but women, in general, including ones with jobs, kids, and even college degrees.

The women dancing to this music like the beat. Something about the music makes them want to move their bodies to it, to cherish it as the soundtrack of their lives. One also hears that some women might, to a certain extent, thrill to the dominance involved in being called those names playfully. Whatever. But notice that what makes her feel good, or what she just doesn't much mind, may be many things, but one thing it is not is "true." I also shudder at the thought of anyone pretending that this way of referring to women—daughters of mothers, sisters of brothers, mothers of children—on one album after another, year after year, is of all things "real." No matter how good those beats it's set to are, it is neither true nor real. It's small and mean, which is especially clear when an aged white radio host like Don Imus trots it out.

Women dancing to lyrics calling them names demonstrate that what feels good is not always truth. Sometimes it is—but hip-hop's unfocused cynicism is not one of those times. A catchy beat and a melodious inflection can tell you lies. Sometimes the call does not deserve a response— even when a black person, rather than Don Imus, is doing the call.

"We used to be in chains, now we snap chains," Wu-Tang came up with in "Jah World" on *The W*. The rhythm and rhyme of the phrase grab you. But think about what a glum, violent image that actually is. It's almost odd how rap can make you enjoy listening to someone talk about snapping chains, especially when he means black men snapping chains on one another. It just shows that beat is not truth.

RHYME OR REASON

While we're on rhyme, it is also part of the dissonance between sound and meaning in hip-hop. People enjoy rhyme just as they enjoy rhythm: it's why Dr. Seuss is so popular. People are stimulated when two lines are uttered that end in the same sound, or when several words ending in the same sounds are uttered in a string. However, that enjoyment has a way of drifting into a sense that some kind of truth has been communicated just by virtue of the matching sounds.

Gang Starr's Guru raps about how he will "relate and equate, dictate and debate" in "Manifest," and audiences eat it up. But the question is what he's going to relate, equate, dictate, and debate about. What exactly is "true" about those sequentially uttered words just because they sound alike? Or, the word *manifest*. It has a certain power, which is part of why "Manifest" is such a pleasure to hear. But is that power something serious, important—or just the kind of power that you experience in seeing, say, a car of a pretty new color?

Is it maybe that the word *manifest* is Latinate and bookish, and therefore is associated with intelligence? Then we must ask, intelligence telling us what? Is it political because it sounds like *manifesto*? Then what political action is being advised? Or maybe it's the overtones in the word from the religious phrase in which Jesus manifests himself. But if it's that, then there is a second overtone, which is that Guru is a substitute Jesus who is going to show us the way. That is, he's going to get us out of our sociopolitical morass. Which returns us to: how? Certainly we're not supposed to think that being able to line up words with endings that sound alike demonstrates a higher level of thought. "Manifest" may be a "positive" message, but it's not a proactive one. It is not revolutionary at all.

THE HIP-HOP GENERATION®

Another way that the resonance of words gets confused with their meaning: the term *Hip-Hop Generation*. People seem to get a thrill out of the idea that there is now a generation of people who grew up listening to hip-hop, who because of this, have been lent a wariness of the Establishment ready to be channeled into political change. But *Hip-Hop*

Generation is nothing but a term of emotion. Let's take it apart.

First, there's the word *hip-hop*, with its crisp, rhythmic feel that sounds kind of like the music itself, with a whiff of anti-Establishment sentiment and a dash of black street energy. Then, *generation*. To people fifty years ago, the word *generation* would not have had the spark it does to us: *generation* has been taken up by the advertising world to target age groups to sell things to, like soda. *The Pepsi Generation.* Or it is used in catchphrases adopted by the media to call attention to books and articles: *The Me Generation.* Or the *Generation X* idea. There is, then, drama in the word *generation* to us today.

So put together *hip-hop* and *generation* and you have a term that goes right to heart of an audience. *Hip-Hop Generation*—feel that punch? I certainly do. But I also suggest that we step back and think about whether the term refers to anything real or useful.

Part of the punch in the term comes from people cherishing the idea that there are now adults who never knew a world without hip-hop. What they cherish is that hip-hop is subversive, and thus they approve of there being a generation of adults who cannot sputter about what black music was like before rap, who never heard rap for the first time as adults and got distracted by the foul language and the violence, but instead were suckled on Public Enemy, Tupac, Eminem, and Jay-Z from toddlerhood through their teens and beyond. No C. Delores Tuckers among this generation: the Hip-Hop Generation is, apparently, a generation raised on bone-deep, unquestioning resentment of the American Establishment, and ready to get mad and not take it anymore.

Upon which we must ask: are they? Listen to one more person giving a talk and getting a little rise out of the audience mentioning the "Hip-Hop Generation," or read an earnest academic writing about it in this month's book on hip-hop from the ivory tower, or see it in a flashy font in a magazine or on some Web site—and then walk down the street the next day. Are the twenty-something brown people you see really part of a potential political movement just because they all listen to Lil Wayne?

After all, the fact that some people are referring to a subset of people as a generation does not, in itself, mean that the people in question actually share the quality they are said to. Think about the Pepsi Generation. What, really, did that even mean? There was no generation of Americans defined in any meaningful way by their embrace of, or relationship to, Pepsi.

That hip-hop is about black people does not make things any different. Are the black and brown security guards, middle managers, cashiers, postal workers, and schoolteachers who grew up listening to hip-hop really just short of rising up against the Machine and making "demands" of legislators because of the music they like? Do they give any appearance of such? Or is it that, well, they all like listening to T.I. and Kanye and that's pretty much it?

I know that the idea is that there is some kind of *potential* for an uprising, a united political *consciousness* there ripe for educating and radicalizing. But then we return to the simple fact that so far, that potential is tough to perceive. These are the people who go to "hip-hop summit" rallies, get registered to vote on the way in or out, and then vote in more or less the numbers they did before. What reason do we have to suppose that more rallies like this will have a different effect? People hoping hip-hop can change America suppose that hip-hop might be changing a generation's consciousness. However, from what I see, that "generation" knows that some rap is more "conscious" than other rap, salutes the conscious rappers in a passing way, but is not showing any signs of rising up.

I suggest that *Hip-Hop Generation* is just a slogan. It does not refer to any burgeoning uprising from the people the term refers to. Scratch the surface, and the Hip-Hop Generation is nothing more and nothing less than black and brown people about thirty and under, engaged in this thing called life in various ways. Typically, most human beings are not especially political, whatever color they are and whatever their level of education.

In the fifties and sixties, black people had a uniquely urgent and concrete issue to get political around: legalized segregation, which blighted the everyday life of any black American. Black people who, under normal conditions, would not have been especially interested in politics had a reason to get interested: freedom and dignity.

Today, however, the issues are much more complex and much less easy to agree upon. They are not of the kind to coax most black people into explicit and sustained political commitment. Rather, they are of a kind that will obsess only a certain contingent of black people who happen to be given to political commitment, instead of commitment to any number of other things a human being might be committed to, such as their jobs, their families, collecting art, making good food, or coaching the neighborhood kids' basketball team.

Consider, for example, that even in the grand old Civil Rights era, it was hardly every black person who was marching in the streets. Of course there were the "bourgeois" sorts who thought everybody needed to just go slow and settle for incremental change. But more numerous than them were people who just thought of the protests as "those people marching." Good, ordinary folks, getting by, buying groceries, raising their kids. I got a sense of this from my late aunt. She was born in the early forties and was a lifelong resident of the ATL, quite aware of racism and, in fact, no friend of white people at all.

But she wasn't an activist—as most black people then in Atlanta weren't, given that at no time ever are all people of any stripe activists. She referred to King and Ralph Abernathy and all of the rest, people making news in her hometown nightly in the fifties and sixties, as "those Civil Rights people." With respect and affection. She cherished the fact that our family knew some "Civil Rights people" (my grandmother was a childhood playmate of Martin Luther King). My aunt was an intelligent woman. But nevertheless, to her as to so many other people—even black people, and even in Atlanta, and even at that time—Civil Rights was largely something that happened on TV and in the paper. She wasn't a marcher. She was busy teaching school.

So even in those heady days, even among people being called "boy" and "gal" by whites all the time, not everybody was a protester. Most people are not political. Look at the footage of the kids getting hosed in Birmingham. Then listen to the oral histories those kids have given us today as adults—as often as not, their parents wished they would have just stayed home instead of getting their butts beat out in the streets.

If even then, when the issues were so starkly simple and so urgent, only some people were political, how likely is it that a "Hip-Hop Generation" is set to rise up today when racism is almost always so much less overt, something to engage in twitchy, subtle, cloudy, irresolvable conversations about, but nothing like the brutal injustice of Jim Crow?

Let's face it: *Hip-Hop Generation* is just a term that sounds good. The funny voices Lil Wayne sometimes flips into sound good, too. Sounding good is not the same thing as changing the world.

LIKE ART, LIKE HIP-HOP

The idea that hip-hop's volume and infectiousness is poised to translate into constructive thought is such an unfortunate distraction that we need to take a look at how hip-hop and its development fit into a larger picture of how art evolves. Many are devoted to demonstrating that hip-hop is indeed art. And it is. But in being art, especially popular art, hip-hop is automatically disqualified from being meaningfully political.

The Monstrousness of Art

Way back in 1937, sociologist Pitirim Sorokin wrote about a difference present even in the earliest human societies between what he termed *sensate* music and *ideational* music.

Sensate music is beautiful, produced to please the senses, usually by a single person: think Mozart. Ideational music is spare and sober, produced to serve a function, usually religious, and usually by a collective: think Gregorian chants.

In Ancient Greece, music was at first mostly ideational: the music played and sung at festivals and performances was austere, focused on collective effort rather than solos, and did not change from year to year. However, after the fourth century BC, sensate music began to take over. As Sorokin put it, the music became

1. More and more profane
2. More and more sensual
3. More and more "human," free, individualistic
4. More and more intended to produce "effects," sensation
5. More and more impure, complicated, with ever-increasing tendency to be "bigger" in mass and quantity
6. More and more "professional"

7. The common man and his affairs tended to be
    the theme . . . respectively the spirit of profanity,
    love, sex, "wine, women and song," the hunt for
    popularity and applause, with commercial
    returns.

Clearly all of that sounds almost uncannily familiar.
Substitute Snoop Dogg's "gin and juice" for that "wine,
women, and song" for example—yet Sorokin was writing
about Ancient Greece! This means that what the rappers
are doing is less some exotic revolution connected with
black people "being heard" than what artists have been
moving toward all over the world forever in modern societies with commercial marketplaces for music.

Thus the rapper has

sought to make his living—and a most luxurious
one—to be famous, to be popular, to be the idol
of a crowd of emotional and half-hysterical fol-
lowers. His creation was intended to "make a hit"
and through that to procure for him all these
things. To make a hit it had to please the public; to
please, it had to adapt itself to the predominant
mass tastes, which at such a period are invariably
vulgar, in whatever concrete forms they appear.

Of course Sorokin wasn't writing about rappers, but
obviously that description sounds like something you can
look at day and night on BET.

Sensate music, to stay interesting, has to keep changing, and Sorokin also notes that "the result of this unceasing change is an ever-increasing trend of sensate music toward something not just beautiful, but *striking, extreme, exotic, picturesque,* and *monstrous.*" Hence the guns, the "bitches" taken only from behind and left in ditches, the violence, the bragging, the coke, and so on. Grandmaster Flash's "The Message," as gritty and novel as it sounded in 1982, now sounds thin and almost twinkly compared to an ordinary modern rap recording. That's because as a living art, rap had to get louder, rougher, meaner, nastier. It's what we would expect. It's what commercial artists do, and always have. You've always got to top what was going on last year.

Hip-hop is sensate music, then. The Hip-Hop Revolution idea is proposing that somehow the music can be yoked to an *ideational* purpose: something as serious and laborious as forging political and cultural change. But that's a long, long shot. Why can't hip-hop be both? Well, for one thing, look at how very, *very* sensate it is!!! Sensate can mean good, of course. But the issue is not whether it makes you feel good; it's whether it can be an accompaniment to, or an inspiration for, hard work. Let's face it—hip-hop is perhaps the last music suitable to such a task.

Sorokin covers no case of a sensate music transforming backward into an ideational one. Not in the history of the world. Rather, the last time Western music tipped the ideational way was in about AD 400, when the rise of Christianity included the inauguration of a new music entirely, stripped down in order to serve God. In with the Gregorian chants, out with the loud, crazy music the Greeks and Romans had been reveling in.

But we are not in any moment of that kind. There are, to be sure, claims that "hip-hop is dead." Nas, for instance, feels that a hip-hop that has lost touch with its roots is "dead," which could be taken as an ideational way of approaching hip-hop. But truthfully, Nas and anyone else who says hip-hop is "dead" are being theatrical—i.e., a sensate rapper, seeking attention. Hip-hop shows all signs of living on for a long, long time in more or less the state it's in now, a male-dominated mix of gangsta and conscious stuff, in which for each high-profile menacing "beef" over trivial slights, there'll be a rapper giving a thoughtful interview to some magazine or CNN.com. Meanwhile, Nas may deem rap "dead" when its founders are insufficiently acknowledged or known by younger rappers, but we all know that seriously fine hip-hop can be created by people who know nothing about anything that happened before two weeks ago.

As to anyone thinking about the old-time Civil Rights movement's Freedom Songs, notice: they were ideational. Think about "We Shall Overcome" and the rest: they are spare, plain songs, meant to be sung collectively and addressing collective problems. *We* shall overcome. Not Jay-Z rapping "*I* Made It."

That's just it: we are being told that a people is going to be lifted up by a music that is really, at bottom, all about the "I" doing the rapping. This reminds some of the

"I-ness" of Richard Wright's and Claude Brown's work. It reminds me, however, of the general nature of creativity in art.

The Primordial Realm

Psychologist Colin Martindale has shown how creativity happens not on the cold, intellectual, conscious level, but on a psychological level that is subjective and undirected, seeking unities between seemingly unlike things and plumbing the deep and dirty depths of the human organism. Martindale terms this level the *primordial*. Much of the "real" in hip-hop is simply this primordial trait that is universal to human creativity.

Painting, for example, was at one point typified by the literal, photographic work of Vermeer, but by the middle of the twentieth century, Jackson Pollock's work was all the rage. Pollock's canvasses are extremely *primordial*.

The primordial is not about sequential argumentation, but is often expressed in a dreamlike state. Thus French poet Paul Verlaine wrote in his *Sagesse*:

Je suis un berceau	I am a cradle
Qu'une main balance	That a hand rocks
Au creux d'un caveau:	In the hollow of a vault
Silence, silence!	Silence, silence!

That's deep—"I am a cradle"? Cradles hold babies, for one thing—our first stage, primordial. But why in the hollow of a vault? You can figure out why by carefully parsing the poem, but only that way: Verlaine was not one for just laying it out in black and white. He was inviting you into his own acid trip, so to speak, and in that vein there were Romantic poets like Samuel Taylor Coleridge who wrote under the influence of opium. Well, that's where Nas fits in, doing "Blunt Ashes" high, or Mos Def's smokier tracks on *The New Danger*.

In the primordial, "references to infantile oral and anal themes are also common," Martindale writes, and quotes Stéphane Mallarmé's *Hérodiade*:

Si tu me vois	If you see me
les yeux perdus au paradis,	eyes lost in paradise,
C'est quand je me souviens	It is when I am remembering
de ton lait bu jadis.	your milk drunk long ago.

Rappers, in turn, more than take care of the anal part: the "back that thing up" routine, that "Nasty Boy" skit of Biggie's about him meeting a woman who wants him to do a number 2 upon her person, or even Kool Keith and his queer, daffy obsession with the rectum on one track after another on *Dr. Octagonecologyst*. Doggystyle indeed.

Then, free association becomes normal. In his *L'amour la poésie*, Paul Eluard famously came up with *"La terre est bleue comme une orange"* ("The earth is blue like an orange"). Whatever—call it profound. Just like a lot of Das EFX's lyrics on their first CD *Dead Serious*. What exactly were they even saying on a lot of those tracks? And what in the world did that "-iggity" thing they did on seemingly every fourth word mean? Or, their disavowal of it on *Hold It Down* two CDs later with "No Diggedy"? I know: I am not even supposed to ask. It's just, well, as Das EFX billed themselves, from the sewer—i.e., primordial!

I am not criticizing any of the hip-hop I just mentioned. I wouldn't have these albums if I hated them. My point is simply that this music is subjective. It's all about the rapper. Sure, on top of this, many rappers toss in statements intended as aimed outward. But so very much energy is devoted to the *sensate* and the *primordial* in hip-hop that the conscious part reminds me of the little square with the surgeon general's warning on billboards advertising cigarettes.

> Hand me a blunt and back up dat ass
> You stay up front and don't pass me no gas
> I'm on you niggity fast
> Before you ever done ast
> But you know dis nigga can last (bam!)
> Dem factory jobs my Pops done worked is far
>   in da past.

That is the first and last rap I will ever try to write, believe me. But that's what most of the "political" content in rap sounds like to me. It's parenthetical. It's not the main meal. Yes, I know there's plenty of rap that puts the "conscious" stuff more front and center than that—upon which we return to my point from before: if there's going to be a revolution, then surely it will be driven by the music that most people hear, not the specialized stuff. In the music that most people hear, then, again: the politics are parenthetical. They're not the main meal.

SOUL AND SIGNIFICANCE

Processing rhythm as truth is part of a more general thought pattern that has been gumming up the works in black America for forty years: the idea that attitude, demeanor, or what we might term "soul" is a kind of activism. This started when the concrete goals of the Civil Rights Movement that had led to the Civil Rights and Voting Rights Acts were replaced by people yelling "Black Power!" but giving only vague answers as to what Black Power was going to be.

The Black Panthers were a perfect example of the new mood still coloring our perceptions today. The Panthers enshrined both a menacing attitude and the "pimp roll" or "short drop" walk—that is, a rhythmic way of moving. There was seen to be something highly "authentic" about that way of moving. Urgent, even. Black men who had things under control.

The Panthers were big on aesthetics: the outfits, the glasses, the hair, the high-powered rhetoric. They definitely had an aura, a feel—I presume that someday Spike Lee will do a big film about Huey Newton, and the costumes and hair alone will be a feast to look at.

Yet the fact is that the Panthers left no accomplishment—no political party, no inner city turned around. They are considered significant figures regardless, and much of the reason for this is their sheer attitude and how they translated it into style and rhetorical sound. Many argue that they gave some children breakfasts, etc. But no inner city kids today are eating breakfast on the basis of anything the Panthers did.

Yet it's easy for many to feel like the Panthers actually did something lasting—because since the Black Power era, aura has often felt like accomplishment in itself. It was a luxury of the achievement of the Civil Rights leaders who had come before. Hairstyles and recreational rage could not distract black America when for most, sharecropping, running elevators, sweeping up, and being maids were the most they could expect from a segregated America. Only when official segregation was outlawed and whites were suddenly bending over backward to listen to the Panthers sound off could we afford to indulge in the idea that sonorous rhetoric, sexy slogans, and major attitude were *something, real, important.*

The Hip-hop Revolution idea is based on this same sense of the aesthetic, the visceral, as equally significant to the concrete. You can see it when people talk about rap in this way, moving their bodies when discussing it, sensing the regularity and infectiousness of the beat as *confirming* something in the political sense. But this sensation is a mere by-product of the way our brains are wired. The fact that the beat is regular does not mean that the thoughts are coherent, and even if the thoughts are coherent, the power of the beat does not mean that the thoughts are *significant.* Nor does the seduction of rhyme.

Associating rhythm and rhyme with truth is, in the end, a suspiciously *easy* kind of political engagement. Thinking of your favorite music as politically significant is a way of making political engagement more fun, more viscerally stimulating, more easy than genuine activist commitment.

Most statements about rap having some sociopolitical potential are based on an approach to politics based on the Principle of Least Effort. From what I see, the whole school of thought taking rap as "political behavior" is founded on a hope that today we can create change with less effort than it took before. The idea is that we are lucky—now we have these great beats and catchy rhymes about how evil The Man is, and they will inform the masses by themselves. Black America will rise up with the rappers' wind beneath their wings and make their demands heard, and somehow that rap beat will make whitey listen in a way that he hasn't since 1965.

Wind. Floating. Easy. Hip-hop ideology is always so easy. Take the idea that gangsta rap is important because it is a "real" depiction of the neighborhoods rappers grow up in. The problem is that racism is "real," too, and yet our society is so hypersensitive to its public expression that when a washed-up comedian who got lucky in one sitcom says *nigger*, he has to atone repeatedly for the media. Part of what it is to be human is to work beyond the "real," which is what produces religion and art. Working beyond the "real" also produced the Civil Rights Movement. "Real" alone is just easy.

As is the idea that hip-hop will arouse a significant "consciousness" in a "Hip-Hop Generation."

It's too hedonistic.

It's not enough. It'd be nice if that could actually be how change happens, but it just isn't.

It's moving your body while sitting in your seat, going nowhere.

It's about quick thrills and settling scores, rather than reasoning, discovering, and building.

Hip-hop may be all about the beat. Real life is not.

BE A BRILLIANT SOUL

*Be a brilliant soul, sparkling in the galaxy
while walking on earth.*

Common's Dad, "It's a New World," *Be*

Some days I am optimistic about the chances that black America will be a very different place twenty years from now.

The reform of welfare in 1996 created a generation of children who are now growing up watching their parents work every day, and the mothers themselves are happy about that. The remaining work is attending to men's issues, and the new awareness about prisoner reentry programs and bringing fathers back into helping rear their kids is something I am very happy to see.

The relationship between poor blacks and the police is not ideal, but in so many places it is healing: the raging animosity of the eighties and nineties is no longer typical.

While some continue to claim that it is a myth that black teens often treat doing well in school as "acting white," the reality on the ground is so clear that black parents around the country are going to special efforts to keep their kids from falling into that pattern. When it began, one may have supposed that the Minority Student Achievement Network would likely be a flash in the pan, just as so many "hip-hop politics" organizations have been. Instead, MSAN is thriving, and its goal is not simply shaking its fist and calling teachers and administrators racists. It has struck a chord.

I am also old enough that there is a generation after mine who are now adults, and I see that the color line is hazier in that generation than it was in mine. Friendships and romances between blacks and whites are much more ordinary among teens and twenty-somethings now than they were in "my day." Of course, the extent of this varies from place to place, but the trend is clear.

Some days, however, I worry. I worry because the kinds of things making a difference in black lives are of the kind that require a commitment to long, slow processes of change. Working for an agency that trains urban young people for office work lends no cathartic payoff. White people do not get their "comeuppance," no one apologizes, and at no point can you give every young black man in the city a new life.

I worry that there may not be a way to get black Americans to embrace true progressivism with the dedication with which so many now have embraced anti-Establishment ideology. Friedrich von Hayek once wrote,

"It seems to be almost a law of human nature that it is easier for people to agree on a negative program—on the hatred of an enemy, on the envy of those better off—than on any positive task." Hip-hop politics is about uniting against an enemy, or about being a Public Enemy.

In the old days, naturally black people were united against a very real enemy. Today, there are black people who continue to draw energy from resenting white people, insisting that black America's main task today is Fighting the Power.

Thus the schools must be lousy because The Man won't give us enough money—even if we can't cite a single instance when a school was given more money and improved.

Thus The Man is on the hook for not providing good-paying, fulfilling jobs with flexible schedules for single mothers with children and no education or skills, while getting the word out to postpone childbearing until you've gotten on your feet is somehow beside the point. Or, rap's version of addressing the latter is to bitch-slap in rhyme the women stuck with the kids, for having trouble being good mothers, such as in cuts like Da Lench Mob's "Ain't Got No Class."

The Fight the Power frame of reference yields more heat than light, in the final analysis. As I write, the NAACP at their annual national meeting just made a symbolic burial of the "N-word" the focus of the event, as if that is one of black people's main problems, rather than something that makes for titillating radio and TV. Real black leaders are doing serious work all over the United States, and I wish that the blacks among us so devoted to oppositional ideology would refocus their energy on things actually happening that are working. It would be especially useful if academia devoted more attention to real activist work, and passed the message on to students before they went out into the world.

Sometimes I worry that there will never be enough energy behind true black progressivism for it to really take hold and change things. "What can I do?" young black people often ask. I tell them to go volunteer with organizations like the Harlem Children's Zone or MSAN. Russell Simmons would tell them to go to a rally, listen to Cam'ron, and register Democratic on their way out.

Certainly rap lyrics are not, and cannot be, policy papers; the idea is that the lyrics will raise consciousness so that advocates and legislators can work out the policy. But even the consciousness-raising that rap is being celebrated for is dangerous, because what rappers are conscious about is being lustrously contemptuous of how the country works, with the implication that our job is to wait for America to turn upside down again.

To many, that is the only black politics that makes sense. And once, it was.

But what is the relevance of Speaking Truth to Power for the black man "on the outside" of prison walls after fifteen years, in a prisoner reentry program, getting assistance in obtaining a driver's license and finding work? Actually, it would be good if it weren't so hard for him to get housing.

But that is a rather specific policy issue. Will there be conscious raps about how hard it is for an ex-con to find an apartment? Not dramatic enough, fine. But that means hip-hop is not usefully political for this ex-con. Hip-hop's two cents on this ex-con is being mad that this man went to jail at all—but nothing can change that. What about what ails this man right now? Hip-hop doing a shout-out to the homies in the pen will do nothing for him.

What is the relevance of Speaking Truth to Power for the single mom with kids who learned some computer skills during her five years on the new time-limited welfare that focuses on job training, and is now doing data entry and hoping for the kind of promotion her cousin in the same situation got? Hip-hop's two cents: whitey is on the hook for the fact that she doesn't have a husband helping her out. I guess—but only in that whitey created Old Welfare that left poor blacks with no reason to get married after they made children together. I assume we won't be hearing any raps about that.

What is the relevance of Speaking Truth to Power for the black kids stuck in lousy schools with black teachers and black administrators in districts with black superintendents in towns with black school boards, where new infusions of money have not helped? The Power in this case is black people, and the issues are about educational administration. Hip-hop's two cents: the schools are teaching us the white man's knowledge. Rappers aren't much for taking on something as abstract, and even dry, as educational administration.

In Milwaukee in 2002, thirty-six-year-old Charles

Young, a black man, was walking down the street in a black neighborhood when a ten-year-old threw an egg at him. When Young approached the ten-year-old, a fourteen-year-old intervened, there was what is called an altercation, and Young punched the fourteen-year-old in the mouth. In response, a dozen teenaged onlookers started chasing Young with shovels, bats, and a folding chair. Young tried to take refuge in a house, but the teens dragged him out—and beat him to death.

A local woman's verdict: "The kids should serve a little time, but not their whole life. I don't think nothing should happen to the parent, either. The kids have their own minds." Two years later a fourteen-year-old was beaten nearly to death near the same spot where Young had been killed, and the year after that in Milwaukee, when black fifty-year-old Samuel McClain honked at some teenagers and twenty-somethings blocking a street, fifteen of them dragged him out of the car and beat him so badly he wound up in intensive care and barely pulled through.

Something is wrong in this. We can talk about solutions. All would agree that the injustices in blacks' history have something to do with tragedies like these. But it is impossible to Speak Truth to History—the past is gone. Which white people in power now can be held responsible for these nightmarish Milwaukee events? Or even black ones?

From what I have seen and heard, hip-hop by its very nature will always focus on alienation, capping, dissing, be it about street fights (gangsta) or hating on Republicans (conscious). It's part of what makes it fun to listen to. And in 1958, that essence would have been right in tune with a Civil Rights battle against legalized segregation and open bigotry.

In 2008, however, that essence is about as relevant to what ails black people as a campaign for subsidized pest control. Sure, you don't want rats around your little ones, and life is poorer when you turn on the light in your kitchen at midnight and watch hoards of roaches scurrying for cover. But Tavis Smiley's *The Covenant* does not include a chapter on pest control, and none of us think the book any lesser for that. There are larger issues facing black people, of the kind that Orkin could not even begin to address.

Hip-hop's "consciousness" is fighting the battle of another time. If there ever actually were a "Hip-Hop Revolution" where young black and brown people nationwide rose up and elected radical politicians set to eliminate racism and redistribute wealth, a generation later black America would be no better off, and likely worse. The radicals would fail in their mission because real life is much bigger than they are. Real life is an America rooted in a capitalist, individualist imperative.

Even rappers, in all of their consciousness, embrace that imperative. The successful ones glory in their riches and acclaim, while the underground ones complain that they lack the same riches and acclaim. The overlap between being a leftist and glorying in being rich is very slight—certainly too slight to serve as the foundation of a grassroots revolution.

In an interview Tupac Shakur tangled himself up in the notion of becoming a "rich revolutionary" (elsewhere crowing "We goin' platinum!"). "We Major!" Kanye West exclaims, exulting in his new fame and money. The only substantial cultural change hip-hop has created for black people other than clothing fashions is, in fact, that it is now so common for black boys to hope to be rappers themselves, eyeing the riches and glamour that the top rappers so enthusiastically show off. I don't see anything revolutionary or even deep in that.

Whether we like it or not, America is what it will always be: a nation based on individuals jostling elbows pursuing their versions of the American Dream. Let's figure out how all of us—rather than a few dozen rap stars—can join it.

Part of "The Message," then, is that it's like a jungle sometimes; it makes you wonder how we keep from going under. I know: my old cassette with that song on it is three yards from me right now. But there's more to a message that will really move something instead of just prove something.

> *"We should not permit our grievances*
> *to overshadow our opportunity."*

That's Booker T., and if you've been taught he's the grand old sellout, I suggest you read his autobiography, *Up from Slavery*. You'll find yourself nodding, a lot.

> *"Militancy is a matter of posture and volume*
> *and not of effect."*

That's Bayard Rustin, the grand old Civil Rights leader who knew the difference between acting up and activism, and watched people lose sight of the difference in the sixties.

> *"Be a brilliant soul, sparkling in the galaxy*
> *while walking on earth."*

That's from Common's album *Be*, spoken by his father. *Brilliant*, in my vision, is not shaking our fists at the fact that the playing field is not completely level. The playing field has not been level in any human society in the history of our species. When the Communist experiment made a stab at making the playing field completely level in the Soviet Union and its satellites, the result was that individual effort and excellence yielded no reward—e.g., a Kanye Westkovski could not have gotten rich—and the masses were resigned, bored, and miserable. Plus there remained a privileged elite.

Brilliant is working out how those less fortunate will do their best *despite* the obstacles that a capitalist system throws up, and yes, even though capitalism has included dragging Africans across an ocean to serve as pack animals.

Making the best of an awful beginning is more of a challenge than just raging against the machine.

Making the best of an awful beginning is, indeed, "sparkling in the galaxy while walking on earth."

Making the best of an awful beginning is showing that black people really do have strength, and I mean the strength to do our best despite what life throws, and history threw, in our way—not the strength to complain in rhyme over beats it feels good to dance to.

We will *be*. Some tell us that the authentic way to *be* is to insist that there be no obstacles. But that is to insist that we *be* in a world that has never existed and never will. We will never *be* in anything but the world as it is. And we will, we must, do it as brilliant souls.

To be brilliant is to shine, to be something above the ordinary. The brilliant soul is unmoved by the idea that we will save ourselves with the comfort food of phat beats and impudent rhymes, because that idea is ordinary. That idea is narcotic and lazy.

The brilliant soul is ready for the challenge of doing real work. As all humans dealt a bad hand have been throughout history.

The brilliant soul will shine in understanding the difference between what appeals to the gut and what appeals to the head—and focus on the latter.

The brilliant soul will shine in letting go of the mundane attractions of payback fantasies.

The brilliant soul will *be*, rather than obsess with what *was* and what cannot be changed.

And in this, the brilliant soul will enjoy hip-hop in their iPod while doing the real work of *being* in the real world.

Hip-hop tells us that *being* is being contrary for its own sake.

But being is *doing*.

We must *be* in the only way that will vindicate our past, which is to *do* something.

Hip-hop, all about just being angry and leaving it there, cannot *do* anything.

Let's move on.

For *real*.

ACKNOWLEDGMENTS

I have largely written this book from my own twisted head, as has been the case with my other ones. However, assorted people have been the source of certain aspects of it.

Thanks to my agent, Katinka Matson, for believing in it, and to the Manhattan Institute's Mark Riebling for insights that contributed vastly to the text. I am also indebted to my Manhattan Institute colleagues Edward Craig and Bridget Sweeney for sending links my way that informed my argument. Victor Porlier made me look more erudite than I am in alerting me to sources on the evolution of art. Michael O'Brien turned me on to the magnificently weird rapper Dr. Octagon, and my brother-in-law Aaron Sparks pointed me to some other rappers I had never gotten around to listening to.

I also thank my wife, Martha Sparks, for enduring my brief but intense obsession with this manuscript, which was really an obsession, of a sort that made acknowledgment of this kind genuinely urgent. Our cat Lara, who has been with me for all of my books but the first one, has suffered as well—I'm back, pretty girl.

NOTES

INTRODUCTION

"Survive": Dan Frosch, "Colorado police link rise in violence to music," *The New York Times*, September 3, 2007.

"Because of rap": Bakari Kitwana, *The Hip Hop Generation: Young Blacks and the Crisis in African-American Culture* (New York: Basic Books, 2002), p. 196.

CHAPTER ONE

Zirin: Dave Zirin, *Welcome to the Terrordome* (Chicago: Haymarket, 2007), pp. 122–3.

Keyes: Cheryl L. Keyes, *Rap Music and Street Consciousness.* (Urbana: University of Illinois Press, 2002), p. 229.

Dyson: Michael Eric Dyson, *Know What I Mean?: Reflections on Hip Hop* (New York: Basic, 2007), p. 86.

CHAPTER TWO

Van Deburg: William L. Van Deburg, *Hoodlums: Black Villains and Social Bandits in American Life* (Chicago: The University of Chicago Press, 2004), p. 204.

Kelley: Robin Kelley, *Race Rebels: Culture, Politics and the Black Working Class* (New York: Free Press, 1994), p. 195.

Indianapolis: John McWhorter, *Winning the Race: Beyond the Crisis in Black America* (New York: Gotham, 2006), pp. 48–57.

New York: Lawrence M. Mead, *The New Politics of Poverty: The Nonworking Poor in America* (New York: Basic, 1992), p. 101 and sources quoted.

Studies on factory relocation and blacks: Harry Holzer and Wayne Vroman, "Mismatches in the Urban Labor Market," *Urban Labor Markets and Job Opportunity*, ed. by George E. Peterson and Wayne Vroman (Washington, DC: The Urban Institute, 1991), pp. 81–112; James H. Johnson and Melvin L. Oliver, "Structural Changes in the U.S. Economy and Black Male Joblessness: A Reassessment," *Urban Labor Markets and Job Opportunity*, ed. by George E. Peterson and Wayne Vroman (Washington, DC: The Urban Institute, 1991), pp. 113–14.

Survey data: Mead, pp. 105–7 and sources quoted.

Economy in late 1980s and nonunion jobs: Mead, pp. 89–90.

Available jobs over next decade: Demetra Smith Nightingale and Elaine Sorensen, "The Availability and Use of Workforce Development Programs among Less-educated Youth," *Black Males Left Behind*, ed. by Ronald B. Mincy (Washington, DC: Urban Institute Press, 2006), pp. 185–210.

Black men's behavior: Alford A. Young, Jr., "Low-income Black Men on Work Opportunity, Work Resources, and Job Training Programs," *Black Males Left Behind*, ed. by Ronald B. Mincy (Washington, DC: Urban Institute Press, 2006), pp. 147–84.

Inner city teens and fast food: Katherine Newman, *No Shame in My Game* (New York: Vintage, 1999), pp. 236–40.

Drug dealers' wages: Steven D. Levitt and Stephen J. Dubner, *Freakonomics* (New York: William Morrow, 2005), p. 103.

Spending per pupil: Williamson Evers and Paul Clopton, "High-spending, Low-performing School Districts," *Courting Failure: How School Finance Lawsuits Exploit Judges' Good Intentions and Harm Our Children,* ed. by Eric A. Hanushek (Palo Alto, CA: Hoover Institution Press/Education Next, 2006), pp. 193–94.

Fryer: Roland G. Fryer and Paul Torelli, "An Empirical Analysis of 'Acting White,'" National Bureau of Economics Research Working Paper 11334 (2005); David Austen-Smith and Roland G. Fryer, "An Economic Analysis of 'Acting White,'" *Quarterly Journal of Economics* 120 (2005): pp. 551–83.

Other study supporting Fryer: Karolyn Tyson, William A. Darity, Jr., and Domini Castellino, "Breeding Animosity: The 'Burden of Acting White' and Other Problems of Status Group Hierarchies on Schools," Duke University Sanford Institute Working Paper (2005).

Rich Boy: Benjamin Meadows-Ingram, "Don't Believe the Hype," *Vibe,* June 2007, p. 105.

Daniels: Cora Daniels, *Ghetto Nation* (New York: Doubleday, 2007), p. 53.

CHAPTER THREE

Nas quote: Houston Williams, "Race matters," allhiphop. com, March 2005.

Dyson: Michael Eric Dyson, *Know What I Mean?: Reflections on Hip Hop* (New York: Basic, 2007), pp. 67, 86.

Kitwana on education: Kitwana, p. 179.

"Urban market guru": S. Craig Watkins, *Hip Hop Matters* (Boston: Beacon Press, 2005), p. 144.

Clemente: Watkins, p. 158.

"A hip-hop political agenda that matters": Watkins, p. 162.

Elliot Wilson: Correspondents of *The New York Times, How Race Is Lived in America* (New York: Times Books, 2001), p. 221.

"Its critics often fail to acknowledge": Dyson, p. xvii.

CHAPTER FOUR

National Black Political Convention: Peniel E. Joseph, *Waiting 'Til the Midnight Hour* (New York: Henry Holt & Co., 2006), pp. 276–83.

Loury: Glenn Loury, "What manner of people are we?," *Booker T. Washington: A Re-examination*, ed. by Diane Carol Bast and S. T. Karnick (Chicago: The Heartland Institute, 2007), p. 25.

Keyes: Cheryl L. Keyes, *Rap Music and Street Consciousness* (Urbana: University of Illinois Press, 2002), p. 229.

CHAPTER FIVE

Orwell: George Orwell, "Politics and the English Language," *Horizon* 13: pp. 252–65.

Ellison: Arnold Rampersad, *Ralph Ellison: A Biography* (New York: Alfred A. Knopf, 2007), p. 507.

Sorokin: Pitirim Sorokin, *Social and Cultural Dynamics* (Vol. I: *Fluctuation of Forms of Art*) (New York: American Book Company, 1937), pp. 531–94.

Martindale: Colin Martindale, *The Clockwork Muse: The Predictability of Artistic Change* (New York: Basic Books, 1990).